PROVIDENCE PUBLIC LIBRARY

3 1116 01043 6639

D0814589

986.2
B8540

15.95

185

Operation Just

OPERATION JUST CAUSE

Panama
December 1989

A Soldier's Eyewitness Account

1LT Clarence E. Briggs III, USA
Paratrooper, 82nd Airborne Division

Stackpole Books

Copyright © 1990 by Clarence E. Briggs III

Published by
STACKPOLE BOOKS
Cameron and Kelker Streets
P.O. Box 1831
Harrisburg, PA 17105

3 1116 01043 6639

JAN 0 7 1991

986.2

B 8540

All rights reserved, including the right to reproduce this book or
portions thereof in any form or by any means, electronic or mechani-
cal, including photocopying, recording, or by any information storage
and retrieval system, without permission in writing from the pub-
lisher. All inquiries should be addressed to Stackpole Books, Cameron
and Kelker Streets, P.O. Box 1831, Harrisburg, Pennsylvania 17105.

This book is not an official publication of the Department of Defense
or the Department of the Army, nor does its publication in any way
imply its endorsement by these agencies.

All information in this book has been declassified by the appropriate agency.

Front cover photo by Doug Pensinger. © 1990 by *Army Times*.
Author photo by LT Sean Corrigan.
Cover design by Caroline Miller.

Printed in the United States of America

First Edition

10 9 8 7 6 5 4 3 2 1

Library of Congress Cataloging-in-Publication Data

Briggs, Clarence E.
    Operation Just Cause : Panama, December 1989 : a soldier's
eyewitness account / Clarence E. Briggs III.—1st ed.
        p.   cm.
    Includes bibliographical references and index.
    ISBN 0-8117-2520-0
    1. Panama—History—American invasion, 1989—Personal narratives,
American. I. Briggs, Clarence E. II. Title.
F1567.B75 1990
972.8705'3—dc20   90-10079
                                                                  CIP

Special thanks to the men of Bravo Company who would not let me forget the soldier's point of view. I can only hope that I have done them justice.

Contents

Foreword

Twenty-one years ago I entered the Army at the height of the Vietnam War. My motives did not originate from a sense of duty, honor, and country but from the fact that I was young, audacious, and defiant. The Army seemed a good place for a young man with these characteristics. I volunteered to go to Vietnam a couple of times but did not make it. Since that time I have grown more patriotic, even during the years when the American government and the military were not the most popular institutions around. Seems like everyone had something bad to say. Time and experience gradually shaped my attitudes about serving my country in an armed conflict. The ignorant defiance of my youth slowly gave way to a seriousness rooted in a deep respect for the values of this great nation and a concern for the soldiers I led.

Since 1969 I have served with outfits that were at the cutting edge of the American defense and could have gone to war at a moment's notice. More than once my fellow soldiers and I thought that we were on that "one way trip" to "destination unknown." Anyone who has been part of the Rapid Deployment Force can tell you it "ain't exactly the most comfortable lifestyle." Entertaining, yes . . . comfortable, no. Sometimes you find yourself wondering what exactly it is you are supposed to be doing. Somewhere in the back of your mind, though, lurks the suspicion that maybe, just maybe, this is the real thing.

That suspicion became reality in December 1989, five days before Christmas. Before we knew it, H-Hour was upon us and we were caught up in freeing the Panamanian people and protecting U.S. interests. Of course, at the time our thoughts were focused on more basic concerns, like accomplishing the mission and staying alive. Both objectives were readily achieved through a peculiar mix of audacity displayed by our younger soldiers and the comprehension by we older ones that can only come from years of experience.

When we returned home, we were greeted by our loved ones and friends. Indeed, we received a hero's welcome because we had fulfilled obligations that we had sworn to honor by virtue of being American soldiers. Whether we were right or wrong is immaterial. Let the historians figure that one out. What is relevant, though, is that we were soldiers, ordinary men who had been called to action much like our Vietnam veterans, so many of whom were denied a hero's welcome home.

I said it then and I'll say it again—welcome home . . . Airborne!

Thomas W. Crittenden
First Sergeant, USA

First Sergeant Thomas Crittenden

Acknowledgments

A friend of mine once confided in me that he suspected he may have had one original thought in his entire lifetime. He contended that everything else produced by his gray matter was merely a weird mesh of ideas borrowed from various sources over the years. Borrowing his ideas, and following this line of reasoning, I would like to thank those who contributed to this "weird mesh of ideas."

First, special thanks to the men and officers of "strikehold," who generously rendered their time and effort in assisting me toward the completion of this book. What began as scribbled notes on scrap paper in Panama gained momentum by way of interviews, photographs, and skull sessions and culminated in a reasonably coherent story. Particular thanks to CPT Bryan Dyer and PFC David Grimshaw, who helped to edit the manuscript with an infantryman's eye.

I am also grateful to my professors at the University of Nebraska and the Ohio State University, whose influence escapes articulation. Although they did not contribute directly to the genesis of this book, Professors Ivan Volgyes and Chadwick Alger have unknowingly inspired me through the years by imparting that critical element of reason to my thought process.

Unfortunately, I cannot possibly mention all those who have shaped my thinking about the operation, particularly from the academic side of the house. Where possible, I have cited references within the text. In addition, I have included a bibliography of suggested readings that have provided me with an excellent information base. I consider them all superb works and recommend them wholeheartedly to anyone interested in the study of war.

I would be remiss if I did not mention Richard Curtis, my agent, who patiently explained the finer points of the publishing industry to me. Credit also goes to Mary Suggs and Ann Wagoner at Stackpole Books who facilitated the transformation of the manuscript from a rough draft into readable prose.

Warm appreciation goes to my family, especially to Vicki, my wife, who supported and put up with me while I was struggling to complete this undertaking.

Finally, to paratroopers everywhere . . . AIRBORNE! ALL THE WAY!

CANADA

UNITED STATES

★ Washington, D.C.

• Fort Bragg, N.C.

Atlantic Ocean

Gulf of Mexico

MEXICO

CUBA

HAITI

DOMINICAN REPUBLIC

BRITISH HONDURAS

HONDURAS

Caribbean Sea

Pacific Ocean

NICARAGUA

GUATEMALA

EL SALVADOR

COSTA RICA

PANAMA

COLOMBIA

Rules of Engagement

A Framework for Soldiering

On more than one occasion I remember thinking, "This is bullshit," when one of my instructors emphatically pointed out the necessity of doing something the "right way." The right way is usually the more difficult and demands greater effort and discipline. The natural human tendency is to seek the path of least resistance, which, at least when training for combat, is the wrong approach. Over and over again the combat-veteran instructors admonished our class in the Infantry Basic Course on this point.

I recall an instance during Advanced Infantry Ranger School when one of my instructors, a crusty old combat veteran, screamed at me for screwing up as the patrol leader on an air assault operation.

"Briggs, you idiot!" he shouted. "You're gonna get your whole platoon killed!" The old Ranger instructor's appearance reflected what he remembered from his own experience. Deeply carved character lines, the look in his eyes, and a hard set to his jaw revealed a complex and Spartan inner development.

"Why is this guy such a hard case?" I wondered. "He is taking this much too personally." Nevertheless, his thinking was undeniably clear. I admired him and listened with grim attentiveness as he explained his reasoning. His lesson had a profound effect on me and forced me to realize that there is little room for error or carelessness in anyone who is a leader of soliders, whether he is a team leader or a commander.

Unfortunately, the number of combat-experienced soldiers remaining in the Army shrinks with every passing year, and with them goes a wealth of experience. This, of course, does not relieve us, the newest generation of American soldiers, from the awesome responsibility of defending our nation, but it is difficult to adequately prepare for a situation that you have never personally encountered. The first time your world shatters around you as bullets whiz overhead, you feel numb and helpless. You suddenly realize that war is reality, and the obscene mystery of combat is revealed. You come face to face with the recognition of your own mortality. At that moment, training becomes combat when soldiers are shocked into discovering the fighter within.

For me and many other American soldiers, that moment of discovery came in Panama in late December 1989. This is my story, and is not meant to be an all-inclusive history of Operation Just Cause. It is a personal account, by a rifle company executive officer, about the men of Bravo Company, 3rd Battalion, 504th Parachute Infantry Regiment, 82nd Airborne Division, beside whom I had the privilege of fighting in our nation's largest military operation since the Vietnam era. It is about a group of courageous paratroopers who, for the most part, ventured untried into combat and emerged triumphant.

As war stories go, this one is probably a modest account, yet I hope it both conveys the viewpoint of the men who participated in this incredible adventure and provides those who did not with a framework for dealing with this type of conflict in the future. To do this, I have attempted to establish a perceptional perch from which to view the overall operation and to provide a set of conceptual binoculars that can be adjusted to focus in on the individual episodes we encountered.

As Operation Just Cause unfolded, the political goals, strategic considerations, and tactical imperatives of the mission caused the rules of engagement, which governed our conduct as soldiers, to change. Each time the rules changed, our role changed. By the time we left Panama, we as soldiers had operated under five separate sets of rules of engagement and had assumed five distinct roles. Each of these roles evolved as the overall situation developed.

Before deploying to Panama we were Gamesters, attempting by prior planning and preparation to secure an advantage in an undertaking involving risk. Assumptions and calculation characterized this phase, as resources were allocated on the basis of what we thought might happen. After we arrived in Panama we became Agents, an active force exercising American rights under the Panama Canal Treaty, empowered to act under certain circumstances in order to produce an effect. At H-hour we became Warriors, with clearly defined military objectives to be achieved by closing with and destroying the enemy. Soon thereafter, we assumed a Constable role as a militarized police force establishing law and order in the wake of our victory. Finally, just before we left, we became Guardians, entrusted to take care and custody of Panama and provide assistance to its citizens.

Before beginning each phase of the operation, we were briefed on the new rules of engagement that had been established by higher headquarters. Each set of rules defined how the following interrelated legal principles of the Laws of Land Warfare applied to that particular mission.

1. *Military Necessity.* Measures which are not otherwise forbidden by international law are justified when necessary to secure the complete submission of the enemy as soon as possible. Military necessity does not justify any measures expressly prohibited by the law of war.

2. *Proportionality.* The application of combat power and resulting destruction of life and property should not be disproportionate to the military advantage gained thereby.

3. *Avoidance of Unnecessary Suffering.* Destruction or injury to persons or property is prohibited unless necessary to gain some military advantage against the enemy. Where military necessity dictates the engagement of a target, weapons will be employed in such a manner as to minimize collateral damage to the extent practical, but in no event will minimization take precedence over U.S. lives.

When threatening situations arose, we handled them as well as possible in accordance with the rules of engagement in effect at the time. Problems arose when we suddenly had to change roles. For the most part we were infantrymen, trained primarily "to close with and destroy the enemy." Then suddenly we were expected to act as diplomats and policemen. Behavior deemed meritorious under one set of rules could be construed as unacceptable under another set. It's not difficult to understand how a soldier can become confused when he is praised for an act in one instance but is then reprimanded for a similar act in another. This is especially true in an environment where hesitation or a lapse in judgment could very well kill you or your fellow soldiers. The result was often frustration, tension, and ambivalence that further complicated an already confusing state of affairs.

Nevertheless, from the standpoint of mission accomplishment and minimization of casualties, Operation Just Cause was an overwhelming success. There are lessons to be learned at all levels of the operation, including the experiences of the American soldier who adapted to changing circumstances for which he had little or no prior training. His ordeal in Panama warrants further study not only as an example of heroism but as a model for future conflicts that may require soldiers to once again act in a complex and rapidly changing combat environment.

This book is therefore dedicated to the American grunt, who is always asked to do so much with so little.

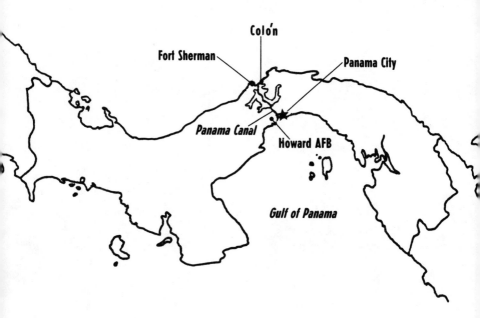

Caribbean Sea

Colón

Fort Sherman

Panama City

Panama Canal

Howard AFB

Gulf of Panama

Pacific Ocean

Gamesters
Preparation and Planning

On 6 October 1989, after a failed coup on Panamanian Dictator Manuel Antonio Noriega, President George Bush acknowledged that some Americans wanted him to unleash the armed forces against the strongman. For the next several weeks, rumors of possible deployment to Panama buzzed throughout Bravo Company. We were already scheduled for an off-post training deployment to the Jungle Operations Training Center (JOTC) there for jungle warfare training during the Christmas and New Year's holidays. Our battalion commander, LTC Lynn D. Moore, who had been assigned to the 1st Cavalry Division during the Vietnam War, had gone to Panama to conduct advanced coordination for our training. When he returned, even the least experienced among us began to suspect that our holiday trip might include some activities not regularly scheduled for units deploying to Jungle Warfare School.

"We have never been closer to going to war," Lieutenant Colonel Moore announced carefully, allowing us to weigh his every word. "There is a great deal of planning going on right now at the highest levels." The room fell silent as the big man scanned the faces of his junior officers with his peculiar, hawkish demeanor.

Enemy composition and disposition were among the items we discussed in our initial meeting regarding Panama. In a nutshell, the potential enemy consisted of the regular Panamanian Defense Force (PDF) troops and the Dignity Battalion soldiers (Digbats), who are essentially a locally organized, poorly trained militia.

As we continued to assess the situation, it became essential for us to use all of our available time and resources to train on the combat-critical tasks that we thought might be useful should we be "unleashed." Subsequent training focused on "Movement to Contact," a technique used when there is a lack of information about the enemy—and, not surprisingly, there is always a lack of information. The purpose of Movement to Contact is to gain or regain contact with the enemy and develop the situation in order to conduct either a hasty or deliberate attack. All attacks turn hasty in the sense that some actions cannot be planned and you have a split second to make a decision, which if incorrect could get you and others killed. The only way to improve your decision-making skills under these conditions is to train over and over with your unit so that, like members of any good team, you react in a coordinated fashion.

Consider the difference between an orchestra and a bunch of guys just blowing horns and pulling strings, or consider any human endeavor for that matter, in which the separate but necessary actions of a number of individuals must be synchronized to produce a desired end. Call it "organization," that twentieth century blessing and curse studied by notables like Frederick Taylor and Max Weber. According to these fellows, human action on a large scale requires some sort of division of responsibility and a hierarchical scheme coupled with prearranged patterns of behavior that everyone accepts as being correct and effective. The result is the creation of trust, order, and predictability—in short, a good team.

For instance, everyone knows to stop at a red light and go at a green one and trusts that others on the road will do the same. Trust yields order, which begets predictability. Every situation, from rush hour traffic to armed combat, has a structure of expectations. If expectations are not met, then a breakdown of order and trust occurs. If everyone decided that traffic lights were not worth heeding, we would have chaos, not to mention exorbitant auto insurance rates. Chaos can also result on the battlefield when soldiers don't know the rules.

Trust is especially difficult to achieve when the human endeavor is war and the activity includes shooting, fighting, and possibly dying. Reliance upon one's comrades is essential for success, but is difficult to achieve when life or limb is at risk.

An innate understanding of this concept compelled us to train relentlessly on certain essential tasks. In retrospect, this training turned out to be very fortunate for us. Confidence is the keystone of trust and teamwork, and the only way to become confident in an organized activity is good, old-fashioned practice. Many occasions arose during Operation Just Cause that required immediate action. Most of us had never encountered a combat situation. Fortunately, prior training facilitated a proper response most of the time. For example, we incorporated medevac (medical evacuation) play, an often neglected part of training; night operations involving platoon raids on mock drug plants; and a host of other exercises to make our training more realistic, in unspoken anticipation of deploying to Panama.

Our company commander, CPT Charles B. Dyer, directed the company to focus on Military Operations on Urbanized Terrain (MOUT) training. Captain Dyer had just assumed command of Bravo Company in September 1989. He is a wiry, energetic man who attacks every undertaking with a zest and intensity befitting an infantry officer. He hates to waste time and recoils from rationalizations made in desperation to avoid some important aspect or detail of training. I remember when a soldier pleadingly asked him if we were going to carry dummy mortar rounds on an airborne assault.

"Why wouldn't we?" sneered the commander. "That's what we will have to do in combat."

Captain Dyer had previously been stationed in Panama as a platoon leader and company executive officer. His knowledge of the Panamanian terrain and people proved to be invaluable throughout the operation.

"How to Attack and Clear Buildings" is the subtitle of one of the Army's manuals on MOUT. It also became one of the most frequently asked questions while we were in Panama. (Almost as frequent as "Hey, First Sergeant, did I get any mail?")

In the twentieth century most people live in towns, cities, or some other sort of centralized community. Urban regions are growing. The increasing sprawl of industrial and commercial complexes compels us to be prepared to fight on a peculiar terrain that has been relatively overlooked and disregarded in combat training. In the past, tactical doctrine stressed that urban areas should be avoided and bypassed when possible to prevent engagement in resource-consuming operations. But since avoidance of urban areas is becoming increasingly difficult, today's soldier needs to understand how urban terrain affects his unit's tactical and logistical capabilities, as well as morale.

Panama has been no exception to urbanization, so for us, combat took on a uniquely citified flavor that is somewhat of a departure from the popular image of John Wayne leading his supporting cast to seize "that hill." Not that the Duke was a bad guy or seizing hills

doesn't really happen in combat anymore. Sure, some of our expectations were right on the money. There were, however, some un-
knowns. One matter we found particularly worrisome focused on
how bullets would behave in a room once we began shooting. We
soon learned that the answer varies depending on the characteristics
of the room involved.

We were happy to discover that the task organization, movement
techniques, and room-clearing procedures described in the Army's
manual on MOUT were quite useful and proved to be invaluable in
establishing a basis for our operations. However, considerations like
the backblast area required for antitank weapons used for breaching
walls and doors, and weapons effects on man-made structures were
learned the hard way. Experience, a harsh teacher, was acquired as we
progressed from one operation to the next.

As time drew near for our deployment to Panama for jungle warfare training, there was a great deal of speculation and even some
gentlemanly wagering in regard to what exactly we would be doing in
Panama. One afternoon, SFC Thomas Crittenden, also affectionately
referred to as Crusty, lumbered into the orderly room cursing and
snarling at some predicament he considered to be of astronomical
proportions. The scene was not uncommon, as it occurred on a daily
basis. Crittenden is one of those great, original characters that commands both the admiration and respect of his contemporaries. He
considers himself to be a smooth-talking, good-looking, graceful
ladies' man. He is, of course, the only one who has this particular
opinion. Actually he is about five feet, seven inches tall, is at least that
wide, has knuckles that drag on the ground, and looks as if he is
carved out of granite. A classic Sergeant Rock.

I took it upon myself to interrupt his stream of obscenities and
interjected, "I'll bet you a case of beer that Panama will be a two-way
rifle range for us."

He abruptly stopped, cocked an eyebrow, and took up the wager.
Leaning forward he growled, "I don't want none of that goddamned
cheap crap either, I want Coors." Satisfied that he had gained the
upper hand, he continued on his crusade as he stomped out of the
orderly room.

Preparation for deployment gradually took on a more serious tone. Items like extra M16A2 rifle magazines, IV bags, and other contingency materials often neglected in training rose to the top of the priority list as "good things to have" just in case "the balloon really does go up." Powers of attorney and wills, absolutely essential for a soldier's peace of mind, were updated and filed.

The day finally came, on 10 December, when our battalion of about seven hundred found ourselves at Pope Air Force Base, Fort Bragg, North Carolina, at some obscene hour of the morning, waiting to board the L-1011 aircraft that would fly us to Howard Air Force Base in Panama.

After boarding the plane, we all remarked how pleasant a flight this would certainly be, compared with our usual mode of transportation. As every good paratrooper knows, there is nothing quite like being crammed into a C-130 or C-141 aircraft with at least sixty other men and their assorted odors, shoulder to shoulder, knees interlocked, supporting over 100 pounds of combat equipment. Then, just as you're beginning to enjoy the ride, you have to jump from an aircraft moving at 135 knots, feel a jolt through your whole body as your parachute initially deploys, and then bash onto the drop zone. Oh, what a feeling! I still do not know what prompts people to become paratroopers. It certainly isn't the $110-a-month jump pay. I suspect the answer lies in the character of the men and the challenge that draws men of heroic fiber to test themselves in defiance of their own mortality. Plato once remarked, "Self-conquest is the greatest of victories," and a man who cannot conquer his own fear cannot proceed to victory with a clear conscience. And nothing clears the conscience like a full-combat-equipment, mass tactical jump at night.

As we flew southward on the L-1011, the conversation centered around airborne operations, and the men reflected aloud on their experiences. Instead of jumpmasters and safeties screaming commands and passing out barf bags and earplugs, we had stewardesses serving us food and drink while the movie "Batman" played on the screen.

When we landed at Howard Air Force Base, on the southern portion of the isthmus just west of the Panama Canal, we unloaded the aircraft and experienced momentary sensory shock as the heat and humidity overwhelmed us. It was quite different from December in North Carolina. A strange assortment of sights, sounds, and smells assaulted our senses. It was certainly greener, wetter, and noisier here than on the mainland. It all blended together into a veritable melody of stimuli, befitting an exotic faraway land.

Shortly after unloading, we boarded the buses and headed north to Fort Sherman, on the Caribbean side of the isthmus, more than fifty kilometers from Howard as the crow flies, and considerably farther by road. As we rode, Captain Dyer energetically pointed out and explained sites of cultural interest along the way. My eyes snapped open as I listened intently, for a short time anyway, to the extraordinary tale.

Because of its location on the Isthmus of Panama, the region now known as the Republic of Panama has historically been an important region for trade. It was claimed as a Spanish Colony by Christopher Columbus in 1502, and in 1513 Vasco Nunez de Balboa led soldiers across the isthmus and made the European discovery of the Pacific Ocean. In 1519, Governor Pedro Arios de Avile founded Panama City on the Pacific coast and made it the first seat of government. The colony prospered but attracted the interest of English pirates, most notably Sir Francis Drake in the sixteenth century and Henry Morgan in the seventeenth.

From the sixteenth until the mid-eighteenth century, the isthmus was a strategic link in Spanish overseas trade with the west coast of South America. In 1821, Panama declared its independence from Spain and joined the Republic of Gran Colombia, a union of Colombia, Venezuela, and Ecuador. Panama remained politically attached to Colombia after Gran Colombia was dissolved in 1830.

Discovery of gold in California in 1848 brought the isthmus into prominence as a bridge from the Atlantic to the Pacific. Under Ferdinand de Lesseps, who had built the Suez Canal, the French attempted to build a canal across the isthmus in 1881 but gave up after eight years, unable to overcome the jungle, financial problems, and disease. "Hell," I mumbled. "I would have given up too under those conditions." I continued to listen with interest.

After the project failed, the French sold their canal rights to the United States for $40 million. A treaty was negotiated between the United States and Colombia in 1903 in order to obtain the consent of Colombia for the completion of the canal project. When Colombia refused to ratify the treaty, Panama seceded from Colombia and, backed by U.S. naval forces, declared its independence. Panama then signed a canal agreement with the United States and received a lump sum of $10 million and an annual rent of $250,000. The Hay-Bunau-Varilla Treaty of 1903 gave the United States an eight-kilometer strip of land on either side of the canal and permitted it to intervene when necessary to protect Panamanian independence, to defend the canal, and to maintain order in Panama City and Colón in the Canal Zone. The Panama Canal was built from 1904–14 by the U.S. Army Corps of Engineers under COL George Washington Goethals, and was opened in 1914. As a feat of engineering, the Canal is staggering, especially in the context of turn-of-the-century technology.

During World War II, Panama declared war on the Axis powers and allowed the United States to establish air bases for defense of the Canal. In the post-war decades, the question of sovereignty over the Canal Zone dominated Panamanian politics. Final agreement on the future of the Canal and the Canal Zone came in September 1977, when Panama's Brigadier General Omar Torrijos Herrera and U.S. President Jimmy Carter signed two important documents, the Panama Canal Treaty and the Neutrality Treaty.

The Panama Canal Treaty nullified the Hay-Bunau-Varilla Treaty of 1903, recognizing Panama's sovereignty over the Canal Zone (which ceased to exist as of 1 October 1979) and granting the United States the right to operate, maintain, and manage the Canal through 31 December 1999, when Panama would assume ownership of it. This treaty also established the Panama Canal Commission, an agency which would subsidize Panama for use of the Canal. The Neutrality Treaty guaranteed the neutrality of the Canal for use by vessels of all nations during times of both peace and war.

After we had finished our historical tour, we arrived at Fort Sherman and occupied our billets, which consisted of four-story concrete and wooden buildings arrayed along the shoreline facing the city of Colón to the east across Limon Bay. Immediately to our west was a large open field and airstrip used by the choppers that constantly hovered in and around the reservation. Just on the other side of the airstrip was a lagoon where fishing and swimming were allowed during off-duty hours. Enclosing the whole compound was a densely packed, thick, double-canopy jungle that was only occasionally broken by a trail or dirt road that penetrated to some place lost from sight. As we stepped off the buses the scene was not all that unfamiliar. First sergeants were screaming out orders while troops scurried like mice under the gun, hoping to avoid any personal attention.

"Oh hell," I whispered to Captain Dyer, leaning forward. "Here we go again." First sergeants have a reputation for appearing where they are never expected and causing much distress among those of weak heart and idle nature. To tell the truth, they can stress out just about anybody within earshot who suspects that he looks like he is not moving fast enough.

A Marine unit was waiting to load on our buses. They had that hungry, fatigued appearance of men under the grind of hard training over a considerable duration. With drawn faces and backs hunched under the weight of their individual loads, they unceremoniously boarded the buses, all too glad to leave the place that had been home to them for a month.

The first order of business after securing our quarters was to retrieve our duffel bags and rucksacks. Unfortunately, the Army issues every soldier duffel bags and rucksacks that are exactly identical, and even when they are color-coded and marked by unit standard operating procedure (SOP), confusion is bound to set in. There are two general strategies for securing one's equipment under these circumstances. The first, and the least preferred, is to walk among the mayhem attempting to identify your equipment. The second alternative, if time permits, is to wait for everyone else to find their equipment and assume that yours will be left. I chose the latter technique.

As I emerged from our billet after selecting a room for myself and Captain Dyer, I joined 1SG Sylvester Butler, who evidently had a similar notion. We grinned at one another and complained about

Building rope bridges across the lagoon next to Fort Sherman was part of our training at Jungle Warfare School. The technique is useful for small units navigating the Panamanian terrain, which is characterized by numerous creeks and rivers. *PFC David Grimshaw*

being billeted on the fourth floor and having to carry our gear all the way to the top. This, however, was a task that the first sergeant was by no means unequal to. He stands six feet, two inches tall and is as thick-armed and heavy-boned as a man can get. His physical stature is a strange contrast to his good-natured, amiable personality. He is married and has three kids, drinks only soda pop, and has never cursed, to my knowledge.

The following Monday, 11 December, we went for a company run after formation. And oh, was it *hot*! We gasped and sweated and cussed. Being the company executive officer (XO), I ran at the rear of the formation, encouraging stragglers and making mental notes on who fell out so they could be properly reprimanded by the chain of command after the run. For a while I thought the damned run would never end. I was beginning to wonder if I would have to report myself. The heat and the humidity were suffocating. To make matters worse, every time someone fell out, the commander would order the entire company to turn around to go back and get him. There was much groaning and sniveling. This technique, however, has two effects. First, it makes everyone run a lot farther because of weak links, and second, it makes the weak links feel guilty for making their buddies run farther. The driving notion behind the technique is to build unit cohesion by forcing everyone to realize that nobody gets left behind no matter what, and that if you slack off and cannot carry your own weight, your buddies suffer the consequences.

Looking back now, I realize that this peculiar tradition is just the type of training genius that strengthens the bond between men who must be prepared to perform actions that require them to be utterly dependent upon one another. Trust in one's fellows is the single most critical element in combat. It breeds courage and cohesion. To paraphrase Karl von Clausewitz's description of the Napoleonic campaigns, the moral factor is to the physical as three is to one. We were soon to discover that the confidence and trust we developed in training placed us at a great advantage over the enemy. On many occasions they broke and fled, where had they fought more tenaciously, the outcome could have proved quite devastating for us. Ardant du Picq captured the essence of this idea when he wrote in *Battle Studies*, "Four brave men who do not know each other will not dare attack a lion. Four less brave, but knowing each other well, sure of their reliability and consequently of mutual aid, will attack resolutely." According to du Picq, unity and trust among soldiers produce courage, which in turn produces fighters. I am inclined to agree with him now.

After showering and eating breakfast, we again had a company formation, this time to pass out what we called "rat piss pills." A multitude of nasty little microorganisms live in the tropics, that can find their way into an unsuspecting human host and cause calamity to the bowels. Consequently, we were periodically issued antibiotics, "rat piss pills," that were supposed to stifle the little bastards and make us feel better. However, we immediately discovered that the cure was probably at least as bad as the affliction and more than once some of our soldiers ended up sick in bed from the pills. Our company communications sergeant, SSG Dennis Lancaster, engaged in self-deliberation over whether to take the pill. "Well, if I don't take this damned pill, I might or might not get sick. If I do take it, I will sure as hell wish I didn't. In the end nobody will care if I take the goddamned pill or not." This seemed to satisfy him as he finally made up his mind and dramatically flung the pill away. Lancaster is a philosopher who employs a good old brand of southern logic.

Immediately following our rat piss pill ceremony we began to in-process. We received the training rules of engagement. The do's and don'ts for individuals and leaders were covered, including items like no cutting across the flight strip, no marching except in columns of twos or threes on the road, and, of course, responsibility for continuous area beautification and police call.

The only unique thing we noticed about the rules of engagement for our training was that alcohol was absolutely prohibited and that we were on two-hour recall. This was odd for a school environment. Some of the old-timers who had been through the school before remarked that these restrictions were a first. Other than that, the Jungle Warfare School's program of instruction was no different than any other Army school in-briefing. The "experts," or cadre, were on one side, testifying fervently that their Army professionalism makes them the "finest instructors in the Army." We "novices" were on the other side, listening to this well-worn lecture and trying to show at least some interest. I remember looking back over my shoulder while we were being briefed. Our air movement officer and some of the other guys were snickering. One of them just rolled his eyes and whispered, "You'd think they could be more original. I've heard the same crap at every Army school I've been to."

One of the cadre noncommissioned officers glared at us and the chaplain cut loose with a giggle. "Love it. Gotta love it," he said.

The following morning, on 12 December, we had our first class, the class on jungle living. We marched through the rain, soaked to the bone, singing cadences and pretending that we were enjoying our little trek to the other side of the lagoon where the class would be held. The only rule the cadre instructed us to follow was not to play with or harass the animals in the zoo or in the jungle. When we arrived at the class, we were packed into a bungalow hut and were lectured on the evil things that could kill us in the jungle. Of particular interest was a small frog that has a poisonous film on its skin that can kill a human in seven seconds if it enters a cut or abrasion. This poison is so persistent and potent that it is said to still be able to kill in seven seconds several years later, if it is left on the blade of a knife. The instructor took a great deal of pleasure when he admonished us about this little amphibian.

"Men, maybe some of you think you are the bad Rambo type," he said. "And maybe you just take out that knife of yours and cut our little friend to pieces, thinking yourself a badass. But let me tell you something. If you happen to nick yourself one, two, even three years from now with that knife while you're shavin' or pickin' at your pearly whites, ya got exactly seven seconds left before ya end up like that frog." He paused, glancing about, obviously relishing the moment. "Now think about that!"

The men sat motionless, soaking up the rain, with cigarettes dangling from their mouths, or lips packed with chewing tobacco, with identical hard, solemn looks on their faces. For a moment everything was silent while every man envisioned being attacked by this killer frog.

We also had a class on how to construct a jungle hooch, or shelter, that could be put up and taken down in seconds. The instructor put it up and then he volunteered two platoon leaders, Second Lieutenants Jim DeMoss and Sean Corrigan, to take it down, remarking that this hooch was so simple that even two lieutenants should be able to disassemble it without too much difficulty.

New lieutenants are often the brunt of jokes by senior NCOs. Most of the time it is done in good fun. A platoon leader and a platoon sergeant have a unique and dynamic relationship as intense as any marriage. It is absolutely essential that they work together effectively as a team—otherwise the platoon is in jeopardy of falling apart.

Generally, if both agree that the most important thing is to train a platoon that can survive and accomplish the mission in combat, then the rest can usually be made to fall into place. Both DeMoss and Corrigan had graduated from West Point in May 1988. DeMoss is from El Paso, Texas, and Corrigan is from Yankton, South Dakota. Both are very competent and committed officers who had no trouble taking down the hooch. They were to earn the respect of their men and play critical roles throughout the operation.

That afternoon the company set out to complete the Jungle School's land navigation course that stretches south to the Chagres River and covers twenty or thirty square kilometers over some of the most rugged terrain and densest jungle in Panama. The Chagres River is also reported to be one of the most densely shark-infested waterways in the world.

All in all, nothing seemed too far out of the ordinary for us so far. It appeared that we might be here just for training, and that would be the extent of our activity in Panama, but we were not about to bet on it. Luckily, we had come down with a "go-to-war" attitude and had made every possible preparation for the unexpected. Our preparations were about to pay off.

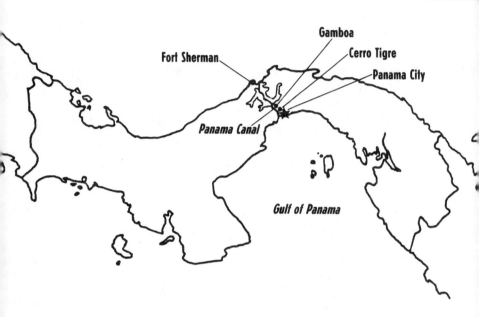

Caribbean S

Gamboa

Fort Sherman

Cerro Tigre

Panama City

Panama Canal

Gulf of Panama

Pacific Ocean

Agents
Eliciting a Response

During the morning of Wednesday, 13 December, Bravo Company trained on combat guerrilla techniques. The afternoon was reserved for our briefing and operations order on our Contingency Readiness Exercise (CRE), otherwise known as Operation Sandflea. Our battalion was part of Task Force Atlantic, and each company within the battalion was expected to complete a particular contingency operation if hostilities erupted between the PDF and Americans. The operation, not taken seriously at first, came to us in bits and pieces. The atmosphere at Fort Sherman became somewhat more electrified, however, when we learned that we would be carrying live ammunition.

Our company mission was to move south by Military Landing Craft (LCM) from Sturgis Point, a boat landing, along the Panama Canal and conduct an amphibious landing approximately fifteen kilometers northwest of Panama City in order to secure the Lapita Signal Station and a Panama Canal Commission power plant. Both facilities are to the west of Cerro Tigre, or "Tiger Mountain," which is a critical logistical facility and supply base for the Panamanian Defense Forces. On order we were to move to a golf course just south of Cerro Tigre and conduct an airmobile extraction by CH-47 helicopter. The following is a brief summation that generally describes what we were to do. Although this information was made public later during the operation, it was big news to us at the time.

THE LAPITA SIGNAL STATION AND THE PCC ELECTRIC POWER PLANT ARE OF VITAL INTEREST TO THE UNITED STATES. THE INTENT OF "STRIKEHOLD" IS TO DEMONSTRATE A COMMITMENT AND RESOLVE TO PROTECT FACILITIES OF VITAL INTEREST TO THE PANAMA CANAL COMMISSION AND THE U.S. SUCCESS IS THE SAFE, PROPOSED DEPLOYMENT OF FORCES BY LCM, WHICH ACCOMPLISHES THE FOLLOWING OBJECTIVES:

1. INCREASE U.S. RIGHTS VISIBILITY IN THE MADDEN WYE/ CERRO TIGRE AREA.

2. EXERCISE U.S. RIGHTS TO PROTECT AREAS OF MILITARY COORDINATION AND FACILITIES VITAL TO THE OPERATION OF THE PANAMA CANAL.

3. REHEARSE A PORTION OF A TF ATLANTIC CONTINGENCY
PLAN.
4. ELICIT A RESPONSE FROM THE PDF.

The enemy situation indicated that the logistics site at Cerro Tigre
was manned by a small guard force, and the Panamanian Explosives,
Ordinance and Demolitions (EOD) school about a kilometer to the
north was staffed by approximately twenty cadre and twenty students
in training. Enemy personnel were said to be armed with AKM47s,
Chinese M16 rifles, and large quantities of explosives. Possible enemy
reinforcements included guards from Renacer Prison, female combat-
ants from the Fuffem Women's Training Facility, and assorted police,
all from Gamboa, approximately eight kilometers to the north. Expected time to reinforce was thirty minutes. Additional troops from
the Panamanian Defense Forces' Battalion 2000 in Panama City
could be expected to reinforce within sixty to ninety minutes. The
underlying implication of "eliciting a response" was, of course, to get
shot at first by the PDF. We were not very enthusiastic about this
particular point and would have preferred to go in swinging. Nevertheless, we set out to accomplish our mission in the best way we
could given the constraints.

The battalion intelligence estimate listed probable courses of enemy
action. They were formulated by our battalion intelligence officer
based on a host of factors including previous operations that resembled ours. The overall intent of Sandflea was to desensitize the PDF
with our continued presence, like a boxer that lulls his opponent to
sleep before delivering the unexpected knockout blow. The courses of
action were as follows:

POSSIBLE COURSES OF ACTION
1. THE PDF WILL NOT INTERFERE WITH U.S. ACTIONS.
2. THE PDF WILL SEND AN MP SQUAD TO INVESTIGATE/RECON
THE U.S. ACTIONS.
3. THE PDF WILL HARASS OR INTERFERE WITH U.S. ACTIONS.
4. THE PDF WILL REINFORCE THE SITE WITH FORCES FROM
EITHER THE GAMBOA OR PANAMA CITY AREA.

5. THE PDF WILL ENGAGE IN ARMED CONFLICT WITH THE U.S. AT THE LOG SITE.

PROBABLE COURSES OF ACTION

1. IT IS UNLIKELY THAT THE PDF WOULD LEAVE THEIR GARRISON SITES IN GAMBOA AND PANAMA CITY AS THE UNITS ARE NEEDED IN PANAMA CITY AND THE PDF WOULD NOT WANT TO RISK ESCALATING THE CONFLICT.

2. IT IS ALSO UNLIKELY THAT THE PDF WOULD ENGAGE IN OPEN HOSTILITIES, AS THIS WOULD LEAD TO A VIOLATION OF THE CANAL TREATY AND PROVOKE AN EQUALLY VIOLENT U.S. RESPONSE.

3. IN OUR BEST JUDGMENT, THE MOST PROBABLE COURSE OF ACTION IS NUMBER 1. WE EXPECT THAT THE PDF MAY ALERT THEIR GUARDS TO A U.S. PRESENCE AND CALL A PDF SQUAD CAR TO INVESTIGATE. AS THE PDF BECOMES DESENSITIZED TO U.S. MANEUVERS, EVEN THE CHANCE OF THESE LIMITED RESPONSES DECREASES.

After receiving the mission from higher headquarters, we began to plan at company level. The commander issued the order out in record time obeying the one-third/two-third rule, which directs a headquarters to use no more than one-third of the time between when it receives operational guidance and H-hour, when the operation is scheduled to begin, before issuing guidance to subordinate units. This allows those units two-thirds of the time to plan and prepare before the mission must be executed. What typically happens, though, is that higher headquarters consumes all of the planning time and soldiers at the squad and platoon levels have to scramble to complete mission preparation on time. All too frequently, soldiers are left with everything to do and no time to do it. This time, however, things went much more smoothly than I'd seen in a while.

First Platoon was to establish the initial security off the LCM when we landed while Second and Third Platoons would move through First Platoon toward their respective objectives. Second Platoon was to move to a battle position and block any reinforcements moving along the road from Gamboa. First Platoon would move to the signal station while Third Platoon secured the power station. We would then secure the helicopter pickup zone (PZ) or golf course for an airmobile extraction. We also planned for an OH-58 reconnaissance helicopter to carry our battalion commander, and a Cobra gunship for escort.

This plan, although it appears relatively simple, was the product of fervent brainstorming by key leaders. The fact that we were carrying live ammunition and that we might actually get into a firefight led to a frank and fruitful discussion. Everyone took a keen interest in the plan, which is not always the case in peacetime. Once the plan was finalized, we executed our troop leading procedures in Ranger School style, relentlessly drilling and rehearsing every possible contingency we could think of. Ranger School is the peacetime equivalent of combat certification. It is one of the few remaining bastions of the maxim, "the harder the better." Demanding, harsh, rugged, almost unbearable at times because of stress, fatigue, icy rain, sub-zero temperatures, and near starvation, Ranger School was the most valuable training experience I have ever had the displeasure of participating in. I used every lesson that I had learned in Ranger School in Panama and only regret that I could not remember more.

As we continued to prepare for our Sandflea mission, there was one thing that bothered us: When exactly would it be appropriate to fire? What was a threat? Fortunately, rules of engagement were forthcoming and did provide some guidance. The following rules, which are more or less recognized internationally, were published and circulated.

RULES FOR LEADERS

1. A commander will take all steps necessary and appropriate for his unit's self-defense.

2. Use only the minimum force necessary to control the situation.

3. If possible when returning fire, use selected marksmen.

4. Without endangering your unit or risking the success of the mission, take measures to minimize risk to civilians.

5. Riot-control agents may only be used when authorized by the division commander or his designated representative.

6. Upon cease-fire, take necessary measures to maintain control and assist any injured.

RULES FOR INDIVIDUALS

1. If fired upon, fire back if necessary in self-defense.

2. If it appears that you are about to be fired upon, fire if necessary in self-defense.

3. When returning fire, aim directly at its source; do not spray your fire into a general area.

4. Cease fire when the threat is over.

5. Allow anyone who is trying to surrender to do so.

6. Treat innocent civilians with respect.

UNDER THE LAWS OF WAR YOU MUST:

1. Treat civilians and detainees humanely.

2. Respect civilians and their property.

3. Avoid forbidden targets, tactics, and techniques.

4. Prevent and report to your superiors any crime committed under the laws of war.

Although they were somewhat ambiguous, these rules of engagement did provide some guidance. But terms and concepts like "self-defense," "minimum force," "selected marksmen," "innocent civilians," "appears to be," and "laws of war" were unfamiliar and definitely required further explanation. Perhaps a six-week course would have sufficed, but time did not permit us that luxury. All questions were answered with the commander's curt declaration, "OK, the XO and I are the approving authorities to initiate." He abruptly stopped, looked around, and made no further response.

"Great," I thought. "I'll probably start an international incident."

There were so many things that needed to be clarified. We could lock (place the magazine in the magazine well), but not load our weapons (chamber a round) during Sandflea unless someone locked and loaded and pointed a weapon at us. The problem, of course, is that by then it is too late to defend yourself. Furthermore, designating selected marksmen beforehand is not feasible, as you cannot possibly know who will be shot at and when and where it will occur. Also, how do you tell who is an "innocent civilian"? Many of the Dignity Battalion soldiers wore civilian clothes. Moreover, the principle of military necessity and the Laws of Land Warfare have filled volumes of treatises and dissertations as far back as 1625 when Hugo Grotius published his "On the Law of War and Peace." Since then, debate on the subject has been reworked and refined into agreements, conventions, and articles from the Hague Convention of Land Warfare in 1907 to the U.S. Army's current field manual, *The Law of Land Warfare.*

We heard rumors of units that had executed versions of Sandflea before us who had been confronted by members of the PDF or Dignity Battalions and had simply frozen up and been unable to make a decision. This was not surprising, as most of the rules and laws were beyond an infantryman's scope of training and seemed to be designed for diplomats and other formal agents of government who have time to whip out the book and ascertain whether or not they should make a decision. The farther away you are from the engagement, the easier it is to pass judgment on what you "should have done."

The situation was exceedingly complicated if one thought about it too deeply. Luckily, Crittenden and Lancaster bailed me out when they hinted that they just might make a mistake and lock and load prior to my going to the head of the column to engage in discussion with anyone. That was the plan—either Captain Dyer or I would move to the front. If the platoons we were traveling with became obstructed by hostile forces, we would announce that we were exercising our rights under the Panama Canal Treaty and were coming through.

Such an incident did occur involving the commander of Charlie Company, CPT Derek Johnson, who is said to have been more than a little uncomfortable with his predicament. At one point, Captain Johnson found himself standing in front of his company as he looked down the enemy's barrels while bluntly informing them that he and his men were coming through. In our company, we finally decided that we would just have to wait and handle the situation as best we could when and if it arose.

After the rehearsals, the afternoon passed without incident until PFC David Grimshaw, the company radio-telephone operator, strolled into the command post (CP) grinning. "Guess what?" he said.

"The chaplain is out there by the lagoon baptizing the guys. Seems a lot of these bastards are all of a sudden getting religion." Everyone surveyed Grimshaw momentarily before the snickering developed into a roomful of laughter. But it was nervous laughter, the kind that recognizes an irrefutable voice whispering warnings into your ear. Humor became the haven where we took refuge during the most dreadful and dangerous of times. We found that joking in our worst moments relieved anxiety and facilitated the cohesion that had already begun to surpass any peacetime bonding.

Grimshaw was the helmsman of comic relief. A former cop, he had been exposed to life-threatening situations many times. He considered himself an artist and frequently attempted to depict with pen and paper, rather unconvincingly, our plight in Panama. After carefully scrutinizing his finest works, we politely informed him that he was a much better photographer than an artist, and that he should purchase many rolls of film at the first opportunity. So he became the company photographer.

Early the next morning, Lancaster and I went to the ammunition supply point (ASP) with the battalion supply and transportation platoon leader, 1LT Don Brown. We drew ball and linked 5.56mm and M60 machine gun ammunition. We also drew AT4s and LAWs (antitank weapons), M18A1 claymore mines, and hand grenades. I was amazed. Never had I seen or drawn so much ammunition. My worries were compounded when I began to consider how I was going to account for all of it. The Army has very strict regulations concerning ammuntion accountability, and the loss of several rounds, a grenade, or an AT4 could result in a bad mark on an officer's or an NCO's report card.

Lieutenant Brown was sweating it out, too. After we had drawn the ammunition, he complained, "You know, I kind of hope you guys shoot somebody so we won't have to account for all of this. Trying to collect this all back up after you issue it and take it to the field is going to be a logistical nightmare."

I examined his reasoning carefully, sorted it swiftly, and arrived at what I thought to be a viable solution. Lancaster and I dashed back to the company area, cussed the bastard who first said, "Hey, we need to

Soldiers wait to issue ammunition prior to our contingency readiness exercise.
SSG James Popp

control and account for ammunition," and regretted we hadn't joined
the Merchant Marine. We carefully schemed and developed a by-
name individual-issue matrix for ammunition in which we would line
up everybody in a predetermined order and issue the entire unit basic
load (UBL) to each man according to his duty position and weapon
system. Breaking down the ammunition and explosives was the difficult part, but once this was accomplished, issue and accountability
went smoothly.

Early that afternoon we issued ammunition and contingency items,
including an IV bag, to each man. We had not planned to carry rucksacks on the mission since it would slow us down and the climate
really didn't warrant it. Extra chow and sleeping gear were not critical

due to the short duration of the operation. We still found it necessary to take squad rucksacks in order to consolidate and carry unit equipment and extra ammunition. It was the first time any of us had carried an infantryman's basic load, and it was heavy. The luxury items that soldiers take to the field in peacetime were discarded as unnecessary weight by all of us except 2LT Chris Bennett, platoon leader of Second Platoon, who for some reason could not overcome his obsession with MREs after graduating from Ranger School. He always carried at least one extra meal and never threw anything away, hoarding the packets under his bunk. Chris is a peculiar but thoughtful character who graduated from the Citadel as a political science major. He reads voraciously, particularly the *Dune* series of science-fiction novels by Frank Herbert. Chris is greatly impressed by his knowledge of *Dune* and the adventures of the central character, Paul, and never passes up an opportunity to enlighten us with tales of the young hero who led his people on a holy war and somehow turned into a worm that affected history for thousands of years afterward. So what. Whenever Chris began to lecture on the subject in Panama, there was much throat clearing and mumbling as his men suddenly remembered that there was an urgent task that required immediate attention.

Just before moving to Sturgis Point to load the LCMs, we held a final inspection and conducted a "forced hydration ceremony" to avoid unnecessary heat casualties. Leaders observed with a watchful eye as each man consumed at least one quart of water. We did not complete the task in full, however, since that requires the squad leader to wait for a couple of hours and then observe his men's urine, to see if it is clear, ensuring that they are hydrated.

The journey by LCM proved to be long, tedious, and miserable as we drifted down the Canal toward our objective. Pulling out his map, Captain Dyer navigated, pointing out the Canal's islands, reaches, and bends.

"You see where we are," he said as he pointed to his map.

"Yes, Sir," I responded, although initially I had no idea where the hell I was. After all, an infantryman is never lost and always knows

exactly where he is. At times he might become temporarily mis-
oriented, which was my case. With a little more investigation I
managed to narrow it down to the correct grid square, which at the
time seemed to suffice. Eventually we were content to chew tobacco
and spit expertly over the rail, watching the birds that were perched
on the river buoys screech at us as we invaded their private little
islands.

Looking down over the rail from the bridge platform, I observed
Sergeants First Class Crittenden and Perez snoozing next to the
Humvee, the Army's all-terrain vehicle. I began to notice that those
two always managed to find the shadiest and most comfortable
spots. I concluded that the reason was years of experience at being
uncomfortable.

Moving down I conferred once more with Crittenden on how we
would handle any hostile action if I were to move to the front of First
Platoon to inform whoever was blocking our path to get out of the
way. "I'll nail 'em," he muttered. "I'll nail 'em."

SFC Jorge Perez was to be my interpreter, since he speaks Spanish.
He is originally from Ecuador and the troops call him Peppi. He is
married, has three children, and has served with numerous units. He
is a good man to know if you need something.

Things got silent and intense as we approached the shoreline for
our landing. By now the battalion commander was circling overhead
in an OH-58 helicopter relaying directions to us on where the best
spot was to land the boat. Everyone plastered himself with camouflage at the last minute. It was the first time I had seen the men totally
cover every inch of exposed skin on their bodies and shiny metal on
their equipment. Nobody wanted to be a target. As we drifted toward
the shore of the Canal we gawked in amazement as the boat approached a vertical rock wall that stretched a good thirty feet into the
air. I thought the boatswain must have known of a hidden path we
could use to climb to higher ground. The boat crashed against the
rock wall with a thud, and the ramp groaned open a few feet but did
not drop, since we were pressed against the rock face. The men, being
the zealous paratroopers they were, began to clamber out onto . . .

nothing, except wall and jungle.

A squad leader from First Platoon lunged onto a narrow ledge and, outstretched, began hacking away at the solid jungle just off to the left of the ramp. He apparently intended to cut a path up the vertical stretch of rock and jungle for the entire company. There was a roar of laughter, and then cursing, before we abandoned the effort and moved on. We made three more attempts and cussed a lot before we finally found a suitable spot. The contour interval on the map is sixty feet. A couple of closely spaced contour intervals is actually 120 feet of vertical rock and jungle. So much for map reconnaissance. Aerial observation provided little help because the way the terrain appears from an aircraft can be quite different than it is at ground level.

It took us over an hour just to move two hundred meters up the bank of the Canal to higher ground, where we finally stopped for a breather and got oriented. Crittenden, Lancaster, and I went with First Platoon while Captain Dyer and First Sergeant Butler went with Second and Third Platoons. We were forced to move along the road since it was impossible to move through the jungle and still complete the mission on time. Every man moved with stealth and purpose like a cat. Alert, eyes darting about, light on our feet, we moved forward. Weapons were held high with thumb on selector switch and index finger on the trigger. The two files, one left and one right, were spread out to avoid too large a part of the platoon getting caught by the same enemy fire. I was thankful that we had trained this way, and every man knew how to move. Now was not the time to stop and discuss proper movement techniques. We could only do what we had been trained to do.

The Lapita Signal Station slowly came into view as we crept cautiously down the road. We heard no sound but the crunching of gravel under our boots and nervous breathing in our ears. The closer we got to our objective, the dimmer the light became as twilight approached and forced us to adjust our interval. We closed the distance between men in order to maintain visual contact with each other. Soon the signal station was in sight, stretching skyward like some forbidding obelisk as we began our ascent up the final hill.

Breathing heavily, with eyes darting about at the slightest unusual sound or glimpse of something unnatural, we reached the top and secured the station within our perimeter.

Relief began to seep into our consciousness and we relaxed enough to drink from our canteens and whisper among ourselves. Faintly, I heard Lieutenant DeMoss call me from the center of the perimeter. I pulled myself up and walked toward the sound of his voice.

"We need to move out now," he urged. "I think the commander is waiting for us at the golf course, but we can't get communication with him."

I considered for a moment, then agreed. The contingency plan, in case the helicopters could not fly, was to move toward the golf course and, at no later than 2100 hours, link up with the trucks that would transport us back to Fort Sherman. It was already 1940 hours, which gave us about one hour and twenty minutes to move several kilometers in unfamiliar and potentially hostile terrain.

Sergeant First Class Perez, the platoon sergeant, roused his men and started them moving back down the hill the way we had come. We moved along at a breakneck pace. When we were halfway to the golf course the column halted abruptly. Something ticked off an inner alarm.

"Damn," I thought. "This is it, time to apply those rules of engagement."

As I began to move forward, trying to think of what I might say, I heard the distinct slide and clink of an M16A2 bolt going forward, followed by another. I was barely aware that Crittenden and Lancaster, who just locked and loaded, were right behind me, to my left and right. I felt a surge of relief knowing that the S.O.B. who shot me would probably end up dead too. Though it sounds ruthless now, the thought seemed perfectly normal at the time.

When we reached the front of the column I observed several hunched figures in a small circle straining to read a map. While I was relieved that no discussion with the PDF or Dignity Battalion was imminent, I was not really comfortable with what I observed.

"What's wrong?" I whispered as I joined the group.

"This sure ain't what's on the map," a voice whispered back.

That was nothing new. Maps of areas are sometimes twenty years old. A lot can happen to a piece of ground in twenty years. Well, here we were, confronted by a five-way intersection that was supposed to be a mere fork in the road.

DeMoss looked at his watch and frowned. "We need to get moving," he urged. Time was runnng out. After some hasty, but careful, calculations ("Eenie, meenie, minie, moe, what the hell do we do and where do we go?") we took the branch going southeast and were rewarded when we bumped into the railroad tracks that led to the golf course.

I kept looking back at our company driver as we stumbled along the tracks at a near run. He is afflicted by a respiratory condition and I was worried that he might be having trouble. When I asked, he waved me on and gasped, "Don't need no pep talk, Sir. Just tell me how far we got to go."

Silence . . .

"Almost there, eight hundred to a thousand meters left," I replied.

I was keeping pace, counting off one hundred meters in my mind for every sixty times my left foot struck the ground. "DDT," or direction, distance, and terrain, is something you never leave home without as a grunt. When you're on foot, navigational mistakes can put you in the wrong place at the wrong time, and it is hard to recover from a hundred-meter mistake that puts you in the line of enemy or even friendly fire. Besides, walking the same ground twice or in circles consumes valuable time, not to mention ticks you off because of your own stupidity. I'm glad we learned how to be stupid in training. Our company driver, Crittenden, and several guys from First Platoon were all keeping pace and confirming the distance we had moved.

Several minutes that seemed like hours passed before a dim light appeared behind us. Paying no attention to it we pushed on, only to become increasingly aware that the light was growing brighter. Soon the ground began to tremble—slowly at first, then building—when someone hesitantly mumbled, "That's not a train, is it? . . . It can't be a train."

Almost immediately a chorus of declarations boomed, "That's a train! Get off the tracks, a train is coming!" Security momentarily went to hell as our immediate survival took precedence over the need to be sneaky and quiet. We pushed into a wall of dense elephant grass, moving in five to six yards, cursing and complaining, while the iron beast roared past us. Dazed and shaken, but otherwise unhurt, we slowly inched back out onto the tracks. According to our intelligence briefing, those railroad tracks were in a state of disrepair and were no longer in use. So much for accurate intelligence.

At last we met up with Captain Dyer on the overpass just before the golf course and eventually linked up with the entire company. The company commander received a call from the battalion commander, who was hovering overhead in the OH-58. The lieutenant colonel intended to land on the fairway. I thought him quite insane at the time but never questioned his courage or warrior spirit.

"No way," I thought. He would be a sitting duck, bobbing up and down like a pop-up target on a rifle range. Nevertheless, Captain Dyer instructed Sergeant First Class Crittenden and me to place an infrared chemlite at the touchdown point for the helicopter. We moved cautiously onto the golf course, all too aware that we were silhouetted in a wide-open field. We emplaced the chemlite after a hasty survey to ensure that the area we selected was clear of debris and obstacles and had the appropriate surface conditions, space, and slope ratio in which to land the chopper. Skirting along the shadows, we moved to a large tree and faced toward the logistic site with weapons oriented outward.

Heavy breathing and the sound of pounding feet behind us jerked our heads around as we chambered a round. A silhouetted figure stood not more than twenty meters in front of us. My thumb snapped the selector switch on my weapon off safe as my index finger instinctively moved to the trigger.

"Three," whispered Crittenden.

The number combination was five. When challenged to recognize each other in enemy territory, the soldiers in our battalion had been trained to respond with a number, which when added to the challenging number equaled the battalion SOP number combination of five. In this way two friendly troops unable to identify each other's faces at night, or unsure of the unit, could respond with the appropriate number and ensure that they could recognize each other as friendly. This, of course, assumes everyone can add and subtract.

"Three!" screamed Crittenden.

The figure just stared at us, then slowly replied, "Ah . . . two. Hey, has anybody seen Sergeant Perez?"

We immediately recognized the man as a new squad leader from First Platoon. He had no LCE vest, no weapon, and no helmet. His less-than-professional appearance and slow response brought a knowing smile to Crittenden's lips, the smile of someone whose pet has been clever. He wanted to be able to run easier on the PZ when he was sent out to deliver messages by his platoon sergeant. So he removed his equipment and left his weapon behind. Very poor judgment to say the least.

The OH-58 helicopter cautiously settled onto the fairway like a giant insect beating its wings in anticipation of descending onto an unsuspecting yet dangerous host. The chopper rose and fell, taunting anyone who might be foolish enough to take a shot that would incite the retribution of an entire rifle company. A figure exited the chopper as it came to a final rest on the golf course. The battalion commander moved toward the linkup site that was already occupied by the trucks that had replaced the CH-47 helicopters we were unable to get. Dark shapes scurried across the golf course as the platoons rendezvoused with the vehicles.

Once the company was loaded, First Sergeant Butler and I walked around and checked with each platoon leader and sergeant to ensure that we had accounted for all of our personnel and equipment. Satisfied after three distinct inspections, the company convoyed north along a series of winding back roads to Fort Sherman.

Arriving at Fort Sherman, we began to turn in ammunition and explosives. It was an accountability nightmare as expected. Discussion, disbelief, and then disgust erupted when Sergeant First Class Perez and Lieutenant DeMoss realized that they were missing a squad leader and one of his fire teams. A frantic search followed to no avail, and the realization that some of our men might still be at Cerro Tigre settled on us like a heavy burden.

Sergeant First Class Perez exploded in anger and frustration. "I just don't understand it. He was standing right there and told me he had everybody!" he shouted.

Silence ensued, and then a voice muttered, "Well, someone's an outright liar or just a plain idiot and might very well get that squad waxed."

That someone, we soon discovered, was the squad leader. With bloodshot eyes and bearded chins, Lieutenant DeMoss, Captain Dyer, and Lieutenant Colonel Moore drove all the way back out to Cerro Tigre, almost two-and-a-half hours one way, only to stumble upon the missing men. They were out of uniform, asleep, and sitting ducks for any enemy retaliation that might have followed our little exercise. The immediate consequence of the episode amounted to nothing more than a reprimand for Sergeant Freeman. The long-term effect was that junior leaders became very serious about the location of their men. And the men made it a point to indicate their whereabouts to their leaders at all times.

I was up all night and into the next morning counting and recounting rounds. When we had completed a satisfactory count of the munitions, Lancaster signed the ammo back over to the supply and transportation ammo NCO. No one envied his position, as he was primarily responsible for any big battalion screw-up of ammunition accountability.

Friday, 15 December, was spent conducting the Jungle School's "Quick Fire" range. This was an excellent range for simulating urban and jungle combat where an enemy can appear almost instantly out of nowhere, forcing you to react by choosing a target and hitting it quickly and accurately.

When we were not at the range or training, food for the mind and stomach were readily available at the little shoppette and library located on the second floor inside one of the main buildings. This was a welcome opportunity to get a cold Coke and occupy a plush chair inside an air conditioned room. You could escape into whatever world was available on the shelves. Later on that afternoon, First Sergeant Butler confided in me that he had checked out the latest *Dune* volume and hidden it from Chris Bennett.

"Here's where I put a stop to his *Dune* stories," he smiled. However, his strategy backfired when Chris discovered the book, read it in record time, and launched yet another episode of gallant storytelling.

The next day we conducted waterborne training, building rope bridges and poncho rafts and using part of the lagoon to test our skills. Crittenden refused to enter the water and claimed that the last time he was down here somebody got attacked by a shark in the lagoon. "No way! Nope. Not me. I ain't getting in that goddamned water. Not now. Not ever."

We also went through a mines and booby trap class and walked the lanes the cadre had set up to point out traps, devices, and indicators. Some of the booby traps were so cleverly concealed that they were virtually impossible for someone who had no prior knowledge of their locations to detect.

A typical lane might include a "Dead Fall" trap, which was made by suspending a large log or rock overhead with a concealed line or wire that was looped around the base of a tree and strung across a path. The unsuspecting victim would trip the wire, releasing the log or rock, which would then crash down on his head. Another nasty little trick we learned to watch for were pungi sticks smeared with the film of that little green frog we had been warned about. Pungi sticks could be placed on the end of a sapling that had been cut down and placed horizontally between two sturdy trees. Rigged to release by trip wire, the fresh sapling, still flexible and yearning to return to its original form, is bent and tied in a way that provides maximum acceleration and velocity as it crashes into the chest of an unwary soldier. Lieutenant Corrigan jokingly remarked that he was immune to such an attack, since he was "well below the normal height of the average man." He then lapsed into a self-indulgent speech on how short people are superior and reminded us that he looks like Tom Cruise. He does not.

One of the taller men countered, "Yes, Sir, but what about the ankle trap that collapses and drives the spikes into your legs and knees? You might find yourself somewhat less than a man."

Friendly argument followed and the virtues of being short or tall tapered off into disgruntled murmurs. We moved back to our billets after the training and cleaned up for dinner.

What seemed like another quiet Saturday evening on the 16th erupted into outrage over a series of incidents described by the following memorandum, which was issued by our battalion headquarters the following morning. We had heard the news via word of mouth on Saturday evening but did not get the full story until the next day.

MEMORANDUM FOR RECORD
SUBJECT: SEQUENCE OF EVENTS 16–17 DEC. 89

1. THE FOLLOWING IS A BRIEF SUMMARY OF THE EVENTS WHICH HAD TAKEN PLACE ON THE NIGHT OF 16 DEC. 89 AND THE EARLY MORNING OF 17 DEC. 89. ALL TIMES ARE LOCAL.

a. 2056: FOUR OFF DUTY AMERICAN OFFICERS TAKE A WRONG TURN AND GET LOST IN DOWNTOWN PANAMA CITY WHILE RETURNING FROM DINNER. THE OFFICERS END UP NEXT TO PDF HQ BY MISTAKE AND THEIR CAR IS QUICKLY SURROUNDED BY A MOB OF PANAMANIAN CIVILIANS AND AT LEAST 5 PDF SOLDIERS. THE PDF SOLDIERS BEGAN HARASSING THE U.S. OFFICERS AND PULLED THEM FROM THEIR CAR. AT LEAST ONE OF THE OFFICERS, A MARINE LIEUTENANT, ATTEMPTED TO ESCAPE FROM THE PDF AND WAS SHOT DEAD ON THE SPOT.

b. 2107: PDF V300 APCs MOVE TO DEFEND THE PDF HQ IN PANAMA CITY WHILE RIOT-CONTROL VEHICLES MOVE TO DEFEND THE DENI BUILDING IN PANAMA CITY.

c. 2205: U.S. SOUTHCOM ISSUES PERSONNEL MOVEMENT LIMITATION (PML) D, RESTRICTING ALL U.S. MILITARY PERSONNEL TO MILITARY POSTS.

d. 2212: LIGHTS GO OUT IN THE PDF HQ COMPOUND. THE PDF BLOCKS OFF THE BRIDGE OF THE AMERICAS AND SETS UP NUMEROUS ROADBLOCKS THROUGHOUT THE CITY.

e. 2225: THE PDF 8TH INFANTRY COMPANY (MP) IS ALERTED, ISSUED AMMUNITION, AND DEPLOYED TO COLÓN FROM FORT ESPINAR.

f. 2235: THE ENTIRE PDF IS ALERTED NATIONWIDE.

    g. 2259: THE "SOVEREIGNTY" DIGNITY BATTALION IS ALERTED IN COLÓN, ISSUED WEAPONS AND EMPLACED AS A GUARD FORCE AROUND THE LOCAL PANAMA CANAL COMMISSION BUILDING WITHIN THE CITY.

    h. 0005: THE 8TH INFANTRY COMPANY RECEIVES ORDERS TO "TAKE OUT" ANY AMERICAN IF THE U.S. ATTEMPTS TO BLOCK THE GATES AT FORT ESPINAR.

Furthermore, the fatal shooting of Marine 1LT Robert Paz was witnessed by a U.S. Navy lieutenant and his wife. The couple, blind-folded and tied up, were hauled off to PDF headquarters, where the lieutenant was badly beaten and his wife threatened with sexual abuse.

Fort Sherman became electrified as our alert status was upgraded. Ammo was frantically issued out as officers and NCOs yelled instructions to the soldiers. Ammunition accountability was forgotten. Soldiers filled magazines and stuffed loose rounds into rucksacks. Most of us had never actually carried grenades into combat. On the Sandflea exercise we had merely stuck them in our cargo pockets never really thinking we would use them. This time, however, we placed them in our grenade pouches. One could not help wondering if the pin would fall out or catch on something and releasing the spoon, result in an abrupt and violent ending. Much discussion followed on the proper technique of grenade carrying. Grenades were finally placed fuze up with spoons facing inward toward the body to reduce the chance of being snagged by a branch or object. The canvas strip was routed through the metal ring on the pin and snapped to add an extra measure of safety.

That Sunday, 17 December, things began to calm down and we proceeded to conduct retraining on the jungle tasks we had not performed to standard during the previous week. Captain Dyer, LT Keith Parker, our company FIST (artillery officer), and I went out on the land navigation course just for kicks. Lieutenant Parker, nick-named the "GAB" (short for giant artillery brain), is from Warwick, Rhode Island. He is a large man and was somewhat less than enthusiastic as we tromped through the jungle. He complained that his size was a disadvantage and caused him to duck more frequently than we had to in order to avoid the low branches and thick vines common to a jungle environment. The course was characterized by steep hills and deep gorges covered with densely packed jungle and proved to be exhausting. More than once we found ourselves backing out of an impenetrable wall of vines and brush, attempting to go around. Keith got into the habit of allowing us to go far enough ahead of him so that he avoided having to back out of any impenetrable walls of vegetation.

"Hey ah, can we get through here?" he would inquire hesitantly as he scrutinized every thicket. He reminded me of a house cat trying to figure out how to negotiate its way around the sprinkler in the backyard to get to its final destination. We did eventually complete the course and went back to the barracks, grateful to indulge in a cold shower and a Coke.

The rumor floating around Fort Sherman was that we would definitely retaliate in some way against the PDF, although how and to what extent was unknown to us. We had heard that President Bush refused to rule out military retaliation against the government of General Noriega. Listening to Panamanian radio stations, our Spanish-speaking soldiers gleaned that the PDF expected some type of retaliation. As time passed without incident this feeling began to subside somewhat. We heard that Noriega had announced that Panama was in a "state of war" with the United States and that President Bush considered the incident involving the Marine lieutenant an "enormous outrage." It seemed to us that some sort of action would be unavoidable now. The challenge had been issued and the proverbial "slap in the face" provoked an inevitable duel.

Another incident we heard about involved an American serviceman who was confronted by two Panamanian policemen when leaving a laundromat near both the U.S. Southern Command headquarters and the PDF headquarters. Feeling threatened by the approach of armed Panamanians, the servicemember whipped out his pistol and shot one. Of course, there are two sides to every story, and both the American and Panamanian governments issued their respective versions of the incident. The soldiers at Fort Sherman applauded the action of the laundromat hero and swore up and down he had to have been an infantryman, probably a paratrooper. They liked this no-nonsense approach of shooting without hesitation.

Actually, it is an old philosophy. "Shoot first, ask questions later." From both a moral and a professional standpoint, it is one of the most intensely debated subjects of modern warfare. Your point of view, in truth, depends on where you're standing when the shooting starts.

Sleep was impossible that night. Breaking down the ammo, loading magazines, and the sound of choppers on the flight strip kept us awake. We slept with our weapons. Many of the men stayed awake writing letters or reading ones that had been sent to them. When I asked the first sergeant if I had received any mail he just chuckled. "No, Sir, but if you want me to I'll write you one and send it off so you don't feel left out. I'll even cut a picture out of one of those magazines to make it real personal for ya."

"Ah, no thanks, First Sergeant," I responded. "I'd rather have the whole magazine." We laughed.

The next morning we realized something was amiss and a quick investigation confirmed our suspicions. Helicopters: CH-47s, OH-58s, Blackhawks, Hueys, and Cobras were arrayed on the field just outside our barracks. It was the first time I had seen Blackhawks rigged with mini-guns carrying a basic load of ammunition.

Circumstances were inevitably pushing us along a collision course with the army of Manuel Noriega. The curtain would rise again and this time the American warrior would step out onto the stage. Considerable time had passed since the two world wars, Korea, Vietnam, and Grenada. The young warrior would be inexperienced and wild-eyed, yet full of the same grit and determination that characterized his predecessors. The rules of engagement were about to change.

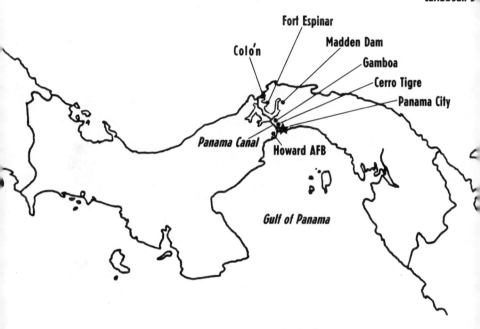

Caribbean S

Fort Espinar

Colón

Madden Dam

Gamboa

Cerro Tigre

Panama City

Panama Canal

Howard AFB

Gulf of Panama

Pacific Ocean

Warriors

Close with and Destroy the Enemy

I Landing at Cerro Tigre

Operational security (OPSEC) became our primary problem from the 19th on. Word came down that soldiers were calling their sweethearts back home and discussing operational details. Some accounts sounded like we were already engaged in World War III and death and destruction loomed everywhere. Manuel Noriega's brother-in-law owned and controlled the telephone infrastructure in Panama. It does not take a genius to realize that he was probably eavesdropping on our conversations. Lieutenant Colonel Moore held a battalion formation and admonished the troops against any further leaks. He was angry.

"Listen, men!" he announced. "We are only hurting ourselves when we pull this kind of crap. Those of you who have called back home and exaggerated our predicament have caused a lot of unnecessary worrying by the wives. It has to stop!"

Realization bit deeper than ever. I don't know what prompted the men to discuss operational details, the divulgence of which could have easily killed them. Usually, when the 82nd goes on alert we cut all communication with the outside world. No telephone and no letters—nothing goes out or comes in that might jeopardize the lives of the paratroopers by making future operational details public. Fortunately, we instituted OPSEC procedures at Sherman just in time, although some damage had already been done.

All day on the 19th we planned and rehearsed. Instead of the Sandflea exercise we had conducted earlier, we planned a deliberate attack on the Cerro Tigre logistics site. We were to air-assault with First Platoon into the golf course using two Hueys, and be followed immediately by two CH-47s carrying the rest of the company. The Hueys would be flanked by a Cobra gunship that would unload its rocket pods just north of the golf course on known enemy defensive positions that included a ZPU-4 Soviet antiaircraft chain gun. During one of the previous Sandfleas the Marines had observed the Panamanians moving to man these positions while an alarm sounded, so we expected resistance. The Hueys were to touch down and unload. Two

squads from First Platoon were to provide initial security and suppressive fire until thirty seconds later, when the CH-47s could land
and the company would begin the assault up to the fence surrounding
the logistics site. We fully expected to go into a hot landing zone (LZ)
and to fight our way up to the objective.

We debated on whether we could sneak in without causing suspicion or compromise. Since the PDF were on 100-percent alert and
expected us, we figured we probably couldn't, which led us to decide
that the Cobra would fire on the way in without waiting for an
invitation from enemy ground forces.

"Yeah, stealth is out this time," said Captain Dyer, shaking his head.
"We are gonna have to go in smoking to have any chance of success.
And it's gonna get ugly if they're opposing us when we come in." We
all listened silently in the CP and nodded our heads in agreement.

Once we got to the wire the engineers would breach it using plastic
C4 explosives. They made a belt charge by attaching a coat hanger to
the top of an empty bandoleer. They could attach it to the fence to
facilitate vertical separation of the wire when the charge exploded.
We discovered later that this was probably the only workable technique, as claymores, grenades, and antitank weapons are relatively
ineffective for breaching fences.

The objective was divided into three parts, one for each platoon,
and a great deal of planning went into establishing fire control measures. Previously classified aerial photographs proved invaluable. We
made sketches and built mock-ups of the objective out of engineer
tape for rehearsals. The first logistics chopper in to resupply us with
ammunition would serve as our medevac bird on its way out, contin-
uously alternating between the two missions. All company SOPs
regarding night operations were in effect. We also brought along glint
tape. Rumor had it that a number of A-C130s (Specter gunships)
would be in the air that night to provide fire support. Glint tape is
used to designate friendly troops. But the tape glows a little, making
you a target for enemy ground troops if the moonlight catches it just
right. When weighed against the possibility of Specter flying overhead and mistaking you for an enemy, however, the advantages of

wearing the tape outweigh the disadvantages. Specter gunships are equipped with 20mm cannons, 7.62mm Gatling guns, and 105mm howitzers that lob 40-pound shells with pinpoint precision. The aircraft's night observation capabilities are so advanced that they can pick out individuals on the ground and distinguish formations, exact numbers, and even weapons. When Specter fires it can spew out over 17,000 rounds of ammunition a minute, pulverizing every square inch of ground in an area the size of a football field in record time. No sir, we would take a chance and wear the glint tape.

Waiting is the worse part. It strains the nerves. The principles of military necessity, proportionality, and avoidance of unnecessary suffering were brushed aside. It all boiled down to "us or them," and it sure as hell was not going to be us. We could worry about the legal ramifications later, assuming that we lived through this. In the meantime we would go in with both barrels blazing, hitting them with everything we had to gain total and immediate victory. At 2100 hours on December 19th, Captain Dyer informed the company that we were going to Cerro Tigre. There was not a big hoorah. "Men, this is what we have trained and prepared for, and this is what we are ready to do," he said softly, yet confidently. "Tonight we will become a part of history, and I know you'll perform well."

Later, as we sat in the CP, the commander put the matter in perspective and confided to me, "You know, we are going to lose somebody." It seemed odd to me, but I too felt like some of the men would surely die, and that is what distinguished this from anything we had ever done before as soldiers. We were about to risk what we had never dared. The whole affair didn't seem quite real. We would follow into a place seen only by a few.

Responsibility is a heavy cross for a leader of soldiers to bear. Any plan can fail. It all boils down to the realization that if you don't kill them, they will probably kill you. Perhaps this is a rather caustic view, yet any other is an illusion. A leader cannot show fear because fear is contagious. Leadership must always exude confidence, as difficult as this may be at times. Courage, in part, is controlling your fear and leading your men by example into battle, where they might very well die. As every experienced athlete knows, too much fear before competition can overwhelm and paralyze you, but having no fear will cause you to be careless. Both extremes end in failure. We went over the plan one last time to ensure that we at least thought we knew what we were doing, but we never quite overcame the fear. The officers and NCOs of Bravo Company adopted a rather unromantic view of battle, given all the prevailing uncertainties. "Where is the enemy? How will he react? Will we be alive after this is all over?" we asked ourselves. Every precaution against chaos had to be taken into consideration. Every element of stability and unit discipline was exercised. Soldiers can be prepared through realistic training to handle stressful exigencies placed upon them in combat. But if they are not prepared or well trained, things will surely fall apart. You must always plan for fear—you can count on it to pervade everything.

Just before the company moved onto the flight strip, Sergeant First Class Crittenden and I moved out to survey the PZ and coordinate with the pilots. We selected the chalk locations for each aircraft. First Sergeant Butler moved the company out and broke them into chalks. Each man checked his equipment one last time before settling down onto the ground.

We consolidated the company mortar rounds, extra ammunition, and equipment into duffel bags that we could quickly drag off the aircraft onto the LZ. We would go back to get them once we fought our way to the fence. Speed was essential so we couldn't afford to carry anything that might slow us down. The company mortars and headquarters element had the responsibility of bringing forward the necessary supplies and ammunition as quickly as possible.

We waited to load in silence. Faces were grim and jaws locked in determination as each man realized that there was no going back. For once, no one resorted to humor. The CH-47 loadmaster for our chalk said nothing after the initial coordination, but his eyes darted nervously as he fidgeted and smoked several cigarettes one after another.

The silence broke when a battalion staff NCO strolled out onto the PZ and came up to us smiling. "CNN just announced that you guys

are attacking this morning at 0100 hours," he said. "On top of that, we
just intercepted a radio transmission from the PDF that said 'Party
starts tonight at 0100.' Now how's that make you feel?"

   Well, quite frankly, I felt like shit. I began to form mental barriers,
daydreaming again as I had been reprimanded for doing in Jump
School as a cadet. What he was saying and the way he said it violated
my already disturbed psyche.

   No one replied to the NCO's comments, but a wave of introspec-
tive despair washed over us. He continued to prod. "OK, who's
scared?" One of the men raised his hand. "There's an honest man. The
rest of you are liars."

   "Oh," I thought. "That's a real macho insight." He was insulting us
to put us at ease, a less-than-brilliant technique.

   I wanted to choke him. As a battalion staff NCO, he would be
exempt from the excursion into Cerro Tigre or any other mission that
night. I'm sure he would not have been so outspoken had he been
accompanying us himself. I wanted to tell him to leave us alone.
There was no need. As he accurately perceived that we were not
interested in his self-indulgent speech making, he abruptly pivoted
and walked away.

   "Now there goes a real asshole," growled Lancaster.

   Someone murmured aloud, "Who the hell does he think he is,
walking up to us like Audie Murphy or something?"

   Our contempt for the battalion staff NCO snapped us out of the
despair precipitated by CNN's announcement to the world. The
chopper's engines were warming up. Adrenalin flowed and minds
focused on the moment. We loaded the aircraft. Crittenden and I
were last on and would be first out at Cerro Tigre.

   The chopper shuddered and the motors roared with ear-shattering
intensity. The ground seemed to move as I looked out the tailgate,
and suddenly we were in the air. Gaining altitude and speed, we flew
south along the Canal, then away from it, making orientation impossible. It was dark, very dark. My right hand gripped my weapon
while my left wrapped around an unseen steel protrusion from the
ceiling. I could barely see Crittenden standing next to me, hunched
over, peering out the back of the aircraft at the lights below. Sweat

poured from my face and my gut was in a knot as I observed streaks of light slice across the ground below in odd patterns. A firefight was taking place, I realized, as I watched the intermingling dance of red and green tracers.

We stood for a long time, with knees buckling and hearts pounding, fighting to close our minds to the incessant, paralyzing fear. Just before we landed I asked myself a question that has probably been asked a million times before—"What the hell am I doing here?" The hair on the back of my neck stood straight up and I prayed to God. "I know we don't talk much, Lord, but if you don't mind I would at least like to get out of the aircraft before the shooting starts."

When I look back on this moment I think of an eyewitness account by John Dooley, who fought for the Confederacy during the American Civil War. He tells the story of Pickett's charge as he lived through it. I think he captures the essence of a soldier's thoughts just before an attack.

"I tell you, there is no romance in making one of these charges. You might think so from reading 'Charlie O'Malley,' that prodigy of valour, or in reading of any other gallant knight who would as little think of riding over gunners and sich like as they would of eating a dozen oysters. But when you rise to your feet as we did today, I tell you the enthusiasm of ardent breasts in many cases ain't there, and instead of burning to avenge the insults of our country, families and alters and firesides, the thought is most frequently, Oh, if I could just come out of this charge safely how thankful would I be!"*

The two Hueys came in first, while the Cobra launched rockets that streaked through the sky and exploded on the ground. The right door on each Huey opened fire at the enemy positions. Then the Hueys landed with a jolt and the men unloaded and sprinted for cover, laying down a base of fire for the rest of the company.

Our CH-47 descended rapidly, the ramp dropped open, and we charged out. The odor of ground burning from the rockets filled our nostrils. The chopper took off immediately as we sprinted forward in two files to link up with the other CH-47 chalk. Suddenly we

---

* From *John Dooley, Confederate Soldier* by Joseph T. Durkin. Washington, DC: Georgetown University Press.

stopped. Troops were quickly coming up behind us, and I could barely hear Crittenden yelling, "They landed in pairs!" He was trying to tell me that the two Hueys had landed ten minutes before us instead of just thirty seconds, as had been the plan. I couldn't hear. My ears were deafened by the noise of the CH-47's engines.

"Next time we'll wear earplugs," I thought. "This craziness might get us killed." Everything seemed to happen in slow motion. Our heightened senses seemed to perceive every detail of the world around us, and we reacted with lightning speed.

Before I knew it, Captain Dyer was kneeling next to me. We yelled at each other, unable to hear anything. Somehow we started to move toward the edge of the golf course, where First Platoon was securing the linkup site. Talking on the radio was useless. We blundered into them and moved into the brush just before the railroad tracks.

We crawled ahead slowly, crouching in the shadows. Third Platoon broke off and moved to the left to attack and secure the northern portion of the objective, the PDF logistics site. Somehow I managed to get everybody in the correct order of movement. We stopped just outside the fence. I could hear Lieutenant DeMoss talking to Captain Dyer over the radio. "We have a guard up here," DeMoss said. "I'm putting Cox in overwatch while we breach." Cox is the company sniper and carried an M21 system.

"Roger," the commander replied. We crept closer, like a coiled snake slowly inching toward its prey. Lieutenant DeMoss called again, this time informing us that a breach of the fence wasn't necessary—he had found a hole in the wire.

The guard spotted us and fled. First Platoon moved through the breach, and the commander instructed me to move Second Platoon through and hold them in overwatch just inside the wire. Someone dropped his weapon, the clatter piercing the night silence.

"You idiot," I heard someone whisper.

"Sorry, sorry."

Crittenden and I followed First Platoon. When we arrived at the corner of the warehouse, the M60 team that was supposed to cover the rear while the rest of the platoon cleared the warehouse was not there.

"Damn!" I blurted. "Where is the M60 machine gun?"

Crittenden looked at Perez and asked him the same question. Perez shrugged and moved on. I was about to follow him when Crittenden exclaimed, "Sir, we've got to cover the back door!"

We were crouched at the corner of the warehouse when suddenly gunfire and the scream of tracers seemed to surround us. Both of us slammed to the ground and assumed the prone position. Tracers flew everywhere. I yelled, "Cover me!" and rushed to the building opposite the warehouse. Now we could interlock fires and observe more of the area. We were ten meters apart when tracers yammered against the wall of the warehouse. Over to our left we spotted movement in the shadows. Someone was firing at the building. I took out my grenades and laid them in front of me and switched my weapon off safe.

Braaaaaaattt . . . Braaaaaaaatt . . . Braaaaaaatt . . . again the tracers flew. This time I had a fix on the source. We spotted soldiers crossing the road. I drew a bead and was about to fire when I heard, "Hurry up, get across the fucking road!" Immediately I put my weapon back on safe and cautiously breathed a sigh of relief. It was Third Platoon,

Tracers go high and streak toward the mountain during a firefight at Cerro Tigre. Soldiers tend to shoot higher at night. *PFC David Grimshaw*

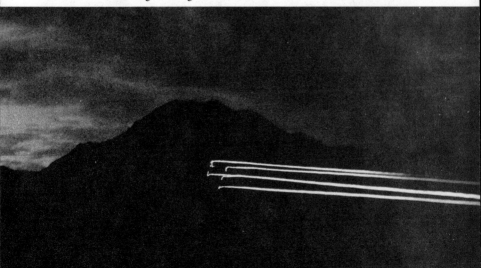

taking out the guardhouse. They had rucksacks. The enemy wouldn't be cursing in English and wearing rucks. Evidently, when they fired on the guardhouse, the bullets ricocheted and flew over the berm that was supposed to be the restrictive fire line between Third and First platoons.

By this time, the attack was in full swing, and the roar of AT4s and the blast of grenades reverberated through the night. Crittenden joined me in the small office building. We rotated security, one of us watching vigilantly out the door, the other peering through the window. The minutes turned into hours and the battle subsided in the distance. Our eyes became heavy from the stress and fatigue. I reached into my pocket, pulled out a packet of dehydrated coffee and unceremoniously consumed it. The bitter stimulant counteracted my body's demand for sleep, which was gnawing away at my consciousness.

By the time the initial attack was over, we had suffered two casualties. A private took grenade fragments in his leg when he mistakenly fired a high explosive (HE) round from his M203 grenade launcher when clearing a room. He had intended to use a flachete or buckshot round but in the excitement grabbed the wrong one from his vest. In another incident, a man took an M203 fragment in the eye. Because of its power, an M203 is not an ideal weapon for room clearing. We did, however, validate the LAWs and AT4s. These shoulder-fired anti-armor weapons are great for inviting yourself into a building where you might not be welcome. The key is to make your own door.

When I linked up with the commander, the company had already begun to consolidate and reorganize. Ammunition, casualties, and equipment (ACE) reports were slow to come in, and redistribution of ammo was awkward. First Platoon had expended the most ammunition, and I was anxious to cross load some of Third's and Second's to them so we could start preparing to defend ourselves against a possible counterattack. Somehow we lost track of the A-Bag that contained most of our 60mm mortar rounds. It was not with the other A-Bags on the golf course, and we figured that it had probably been left on the aircraft. In all the excitement no one had dragged it off as we had planned.

"XO," said the commander, "take the engineers out with a squad from Second and set them in a blocking position at the three-way intersection to the west."

"Airborne, Sir! Which squad is it?"

"Take Sergeant Potts's squad. Stop any and all traffic that tries to go north or south!"

SGT Jeffrey Potts, an infantry squad leader for Second Platoon, and the engineer squad leader rounded up their men and we moved out to the intersection.

The intersection was quite defensible, as it sat upon a hilltop overlooking the entire area. The roads were carved into the rock and earth, creating natural traps for unsuspecting motorists. Prior training came in handy while conducting our mission and terrain analysis. One fork led to the south toward Fort Clayton and Panama City. The other two led to the north and west toward Gamboa.

Since Operation Just Cause was a combined and coordinated operation, we knew that American forces had probably hit everywhere all at once. This meant that the enemy could come from any direction when fleeing the scene of their defeat. Consequently, we employed the engineers' 90mm recoilless rifle in a primary, supplementary, and alternate capacity. We did the same for the M249 SAWs and AT4s. We had a good observation post on a hilltop next to the intersection and could see a long way off in every direction. We hot-wired some cars from the logistics compound and used them as obstacles to block traffic. This created kill zones that were augmented by the steep embankments rising up along both sides of the roads.

Anyone approaching would be caught between interlocking fire from at least two directions, one of which was from above on the high ground. Any attempt to dismount would be handled by the claymores we had set up. There was only so much room between the cliffs on either side of the roads. In effect, this would channelize the enemy and prevent them from running anywhere except into the blast of thousands of BBs propelled by C4 as the claymore exploded.

Morning was imminent as the first rays of sunlight crept over the horizon. I made my way back toward the rest of the company, leaving the two squad leaders to secure the intersection. We were afforded temporary reprieve in the early dawn. As I passed by the men, I observed the sunken eyes and taut faces after our first firefight. Some were smoking and talking quietly, while others just stared off into nothingness, overwhelmed by the night's events.

We had little concern for the rest of our battalion, or, for that matter, American forces in general. The typical soldier is unable to grasp the scope of an operation like Just Cause. His attention is focused on the particular small part he is involved in. Fighting was occurring everywhere throughout Panama with separate units struggling with their own respective objectives, and with men fearing and sometimes dying their own deaths. Eventually, it is all pieced together and the big picture emerges. But while politicians assess the aftermath of war and officers evaluate battles, the grunt judges combat from a uniquely personal perspective.

He is afraid and worries that his fear be manifest through acts that would be construed by his comrades as cowardice. Most men do not aspire to be heroes, but they also do not want to be considered unworthy of their present company. Hesitantly, while warily eyeing one another, they reconstruct the battle among themselves. Caution prevails as they comment upon each other's actions. They are careful to hide the disdain they feel for those who make convenient excuses, realizing, deep inside themselves, that they too felt all-consuming fear. Looking back, they realize that they could have, and perhaps should have, done something differently, but primordial fear overwhelmed any shame they may have felt at the time. Afterward, remorse and guilt, however slight, prompt them to justify themselves and others.

In actuality, this exercise is an informal after-action review in which each man resolves to improve his performance in the next confrontation. Just being there indicates that they are for the most part men of courage. Talking about it in grim reflection reveals that they are also professionals.

II Where Were You at H-Hour?

"Where were you at H-Hour?" is a question coined by our battalion commander that can be answered in as many different ways as there were American units in Panama. The 3rd Battalion, 504th Parachute Infantry Regiment, was spread throughout the country, operating as separate companies. At forty-four by twenty-two kilometers, our battalion's sector, AO South, was larger than all the other American forces sectors combined. Because our forces would be so spread out, reinforcements would not be expected. Task Force 3-504 conducted three simultaneous air assaults, into Cerro Tigre, Gamboa, and Renacer Prison, along with two separate mounted missions into Fort Espinar and Madden Dam. The intricate and complex nature of the operation demanded that all parts of the battalion mission be executed simultaneously and precisely, with the utmost violence. Complete submission of the enemy must be secured rapidly with overwhelming firepower. Any mutually reinforcing actions by the enemy that lead to a successful concentration of forces at any one of the battalion's targets could present difficulties to the company assigned to take it out.

Everyone knew what had to be done—"Close with and destroy the enemy."

A platoon from Delta Company established a roadblock just outside the Coco Solo Hospital. LT Matt Miller and his platoon sergeant procured two buses and positioned them so that there was just enough space for one vehicle to pass at a time. Engineers worked fervently behind the buses to build an obstacle of triple-strand concertina wire.

A rusty old van squeaked ominously to a halt just outside the roadblock. The platoon sergeant quickly told the occupants, in Spanish, to leave or they would "surely die." Almost before he finished uttering his warning, two cars raced forward and attempted to breech the Delta defense. Lieutenant Miller shouldered his weapon and fired three rounds, but it was too late to stop them. The whole platoon cut loose with their weapons, including two .50 caliber machine guns. Screeching tires, the sound of broken glass, and the steady hammering of the .50 caliber filled the air. Two vehicles were blown apart, their PDF occupants killed instantly. The third car somehow managed to spin around and speed away in the other direction.

The fight raged everywhere at H-Hour. Three Hueys, two OH-58s, and a Cobra gunship sped through the night to Renacer Prison

This van failed to halt after being warned at the Delta Company roadblock set up by LT Matt Miller's platoon outside Coco Solo. The PDF occupants were killed instantly. *LT Matt Miller*

on a rescue mission by Charlie Company. The low-flying choppers hovered momentarily over the Canal just southeast of the prison before rising over the high ground, like giant birds of prey poised for the kill. Suddenly they plummeted, pouring a barrage of lead onto pre-selected targets, including the guardhouses, offices, and prison headquarters. The soldiers discovered that firing an M203 grenade launcher from a chopper is tricky business as the rotor wash deflected the rounds downward prematurely and caused them to fall short of their intended targets. They also had trouble controlling the panicking door gunners. Evidently fire control measures coordinated with the pilots at the Air Movement Conference (AMC) didn't filter down to the gunners.

The first Huey veered off to the right, landed in the northern section of the compound, ejected the battalion scouts, and lifted off again immediately.

Team Oswalt from Charlie Company filled the other two Hueys that plunged into the center of the prison compound with right door guns blazing. Twenty-two men defied their terror and leapt from the skids, shooting as they sprinted toward their targets. Staff Sergeant Wagner, an engineer, inched forward under the fiery dance of tracer rounds overhead to the prison door entrance and rapidly assessed the situation. His security man had been hit in the arm. Blood spurted from the gaping wound. Someone screamed for a medic. Wagner, gritting his teeth, crawled over broken glass and gravel to the double doors and hastily placed three one-pound blocks of C4 explosives at the prison entrance.

He pulled the M60 fuze igniter and dashed for cover. A deafening roar followed as the explosion destroyed the entrance. American soldiers rushed into the prison through the smoke and shrapnel to clear the opposition away and liberate the terrified prisoners.

Meanwhile, the rest of Charlie Company landed at the docks and charged off the LCMs toward the southeastern corner of the prison complex where most of the resistance was expected. They could hear Team Oswalt slamming into enemy resistance as they struggled to secure the prison to prevent a hostage situation from developing.

Bullets spewed forth from a guardhouse to the south. LT Chuck Broadus, a platoon leader from Charlie Company, urgently dispatched a squad to suppress the enemy. The rest of his men blundered into a cyclone fence that separated them from the office and headquarters building. The fence was unexpected and presented some difficulties. It should have been a Priority Intelligence Requirement (PIR). PFC Derrick Webster and SPC Charles Ross attempted to breach the fence using claymores and grenades, but to no avail. They inched forward again, rounds sizzling overhead and sparks flying as they cut the wire with their bayonets.

Suddenly, Broadus's platoon punched through. They continued to clear all the surrounding buildings, taking nineteen prisoners of war and wounding four enemy soldiers. By 0700 things began to settle down as Charlie Company went into its consolidation and reorganization phase of the attack. In the end they freed sixty-four prisoners from the prison, killed five enemy soldiers, and wounded and captured twenty-two.

The composite platoon that was part of Task Force Espinar and commanded by MAJ Frank Newell was organized for action by CPT Matthew Halder, a former rifle company commander in the battalion and now Headquarters Company commander. The Headquarters Company crowd of clerks, cooks, and mechanics was also forced to assume its primary role as infantrymen. At H-Hour they performed well, accomplishing their mission and capturing thirty-four POWs. The key to their success, as with the rest of the battalion, was the opportunity to conduct rehearsals on or near the same terrain on which they fought.

Meanwhile, Alpha Company, commanded by CPT Peter Boylan, was struggling to secure three separate objectives at Gamboa, a town

Captured prisoners of war wait outside Renacer Prison after Charlie Company's attack during H-Hour. POWs were usually secured until they could be evacuated to detainee camps. *LT Chuck Broadus*

just to the north of Cerro Tigre along the major road that parallels the Panama Canal. Its mission was complicated by an obligation to consider collateral damage and American citizens who lived in the area. First Platoon had the responsibility to secure the forest ranger headquarters used by the PDF to train recruits. Second Platoon attacked the Gamboa Police Station and established a blocking position on the bridge that led to Renacer Prison. Third Platoon seized the Fuffem Womens' Training Facility where females were schooled in the art of counterintelligence.

At H-Hour, Alpha Company air-assaulted into LZ vulture, or McGrath field, which was located in the center of the three platoon objectives. The LZ was hot and they received a tremendous volley of fire as the choppers dropped onto the ground. Four files from First Platoon, led by LT Jeff Agrella, burst off the ramp of the CH-47 and headed toward the ranger headquarters, which was located on a hilltop up a 70-degree vertical slope. "The men had to literally climb on all fours to get up the cliff in the blackness of night," reflected Lieutenant Agrella. They broke the crest of the hill with aching lungs and burning muscles, exhausted from the torturous climb, only to be confronted by yet another obstacle. A fence barred their path. Undaunted, they hacked their way through, maneuvering around several houses and taking up positions just short of the objective.

SSG Joseph Morely occupied a support position just inside the breezeway of a house that he thought was occupied by Panamanians. Suddenly he discovered that his intelligence brief was not quite accurate. An overly curious American citizen sauntered onto the patio and bellowed indignantly, "What's going on? Who are you?"

Staff Sergeant Morely, astonished by the man's suicidal audacity, yelled, "Get back in your house! Stay close to the floor. You are in danger of losing your life!"

Momentary hesitation on the part of the bathrobed hero elicited yet another response from one of the men. "We're the 82nd Airborne Division, and we're using your breezeway!"

Suddenly enlightened, the American grinned like a fellow conspirator as he rapidly retreated. "Oh, okay. Got ya!"

For about one minute, First Platoon poured devastating machine gun, M203, and rifle fire into the rangers headquarters building.

They suffered four friendly casualties before they assaulted the objective, barely missing the enemy who escaped out the back through the American neighborhood that had been identified as a no-fire zone. Blood trails were everywhere; the soldiers were told later by some of the locals that the Panamanian soldiers had desperately dragged out their casualties.

Alpha Company was by no means the only unit that had difficulty with escaping enemy soldiers. One of the lessons we learned as a battalion focused upon the necessity of isolating our objective. Easy in theory, this principle is much more difficult to practice in combat. This is particularly true if the intent is to allow a trapped enemy some reprieve or opportunity for surrender. Our battalion commander, while addressing the officers during an after-action review, reflected on this point. "Before you give the enemy a chance to surrender you must absolutely dominate the situation," he instructed.

I believe each commander thought about isolating his respective objective, but the essential countervailing consideration for each was time. Speed was critical and taking time to isolate the targets might have assuaged the intended shock effect. The mission analysis determines whether it is necessary to kill the enemy or just push him off some piece of key terrain. The problem with the latter is that it provides the enemy with an opportunity for reprieve and reprisal. As a schoolboy, I recall once witnessing a fistfight between two feisty rivals. The larger of the two, being generous and somewhat good-natured, sat upon the chest of his foe and made him promise that if he let him up, the smaller boy would stop fighting and acknowledge his defeat. He quickly realized his mistake when the smaller boy, after getting up, picked up a stick and attacked his opponent from the rear, braining him into submission.

In any event, after things quieted down SGT Christopher Thompson, an Alpha Company team leader, noticed that his leg was bleeding. He had been hit on the LZ without feeling a thing and had charged up the hill with his fellows. He apparently thought he had "banged his leg" on the side of the chopper when he ran off the ramp. He was evacuated and taken to the hospital. He found out that the medical experts planned to fly him back on the next C-141 to the

States, where they would operate and pull the fragments out of his leg. Not wishing to miss an event of epic proportions, he escaped, commandeering a weapon and some equipment on his way out of the hospital. He then traveled by whatever means he could find to rejoin his company. He was temporarily declared one of the American MIAs. He finished the operation but had to clean and rebandage his leg every day.

Panama was being enveloped by American soldiers, and everywhere unsung heroes were performing deeds of valor and determination. Our experience was by no means unique and other units were probably engaged in actions that were similar to or more severe than ours. The 75th Ranger Regiment, commanded by COL Buck Kernan, a former 3/504 Battalion commander with the 82nd, conducted two separate airborne assaults onto Tocumen-Torrijos Airport and Rio Hato, home of the 6th and 7th PDF companies. As the fleet of C-130 aircraft slowed to jump speed over the Rio Hato, they began to take fire. A weapons squad leader on the jump described the initial assault as a "bloody brawl." Streams of tracers climbed into the night as he floated to the ground. He was struggling to get out of his parachute harness when he saw a Cadillac moving toward him.

"I thought it was over for me until out of nowhere an M249 SAW gunner charged the vehicle, spraying the shit out of it," he said afterward.

The PDF refused to surrender and the Rangers advanced, building by building, methodically exacting enemy casualties. The fighting continued as the PDF, refusing to give up, withdrew and hit again and again in savage building-to-building fighting. After it was over, thousands of assault rifles, numerous ZPU4s, machine guns, armored vehicles, and rocket launchers were captured.

Other elements from the 82nd Airborne Division, commanded by MG James H. Johnson Jr., included 1st and 2nd Battalions of the 504th Parachute Infantry Regiment, augmented by the 4th Battalion of the 325th Regiment. They jumped, led by Major General Johnson, onto Tocumen-Torrijos Airport, assembled, and moved out to separate objectives. The 82nd successfully added overwhelming firepower and much needed combat sustainment through enormous airlift capabilities. Problems arose, however, even before the 82nd left the mainland. Planes were delayed by an ice storm at Pope Air Force Base. Deicing equipment was available but the process was slow. Furthermore, several hundred bullet-launching grunts were allegedly bumped from the aircraft by senior officers from Division and Corps, who supposedly just "had to go." Soldiers claimed they actually had to de-rig and get off the aircraft so some badge-seekers could slap a patch on their right shoulders. Men and equipment jumped onto the Panamanian airfield in five different sorties over a three-hour period. Soldiers aboard the aircraft also report that several aircraft veered off the drop heading at the last minute to avoid enemy ground fire. Consequently, some soldiers and equipment were dropped onto a marshy area just to the east of the airfield. Nevertheless, the highly trained unit overcame these difficulties and executed the mission superbly.

After assembling, the 1st Battalion secured a PDF installation at Tinajitas while 2nd Battalion seized a Panamanian Army barracks at Panama Viejo. Elements from 2nd Battalion rescued twenty-nine Americans, many of whom were journalists, who were being held at gunpoint in the luxurious Marriott Hotel in Panama City. Apparently guests cheered when American soldiers fought their way to the hotel. LTC Harry Axson, the battalion commander, is purported to have received direct orders from Secretary of State James Baker III to secure the hotel within three hours. They did it, but three American troops were wounded during the episode.

A company from 4-6th Infantry Regiment of the 5th Mechanized Division out of Fort Polk rolled out of the Curundu housing area at H-Hour in an M113 armored personnel carrier. "We were constantly ambushed along the route to the Comandancia," a sergeant recalled. "When we arrived we dismounted and immediately engaged the enemy who lobbed 122mm mortar rounds at us. The whole place was on fire."

A stalemate ensued until daybreak when the 82nd's Sheridan tanks pulverized the PDF headquarters with their 152mm guns from Ancon Hill. This was quickly followed by Hell Fire missiles launched from Apache helicopters hovering over the Pacific. The 5th ID grunts along with a reinforced Ranger platoon stormed the building and overcame the remaining enemy resistance.

Not everything went as planned, however. Allegedly, an A-C130 Specter gunship accidentally wounded twenty-three American soldiers on the initial assault. Charlie Company also shot down two unmarked helicopters that came in after the initial assault. There were not supposed to be any friendly aircraft in the area. The guys on board survived, strolled into the Comandancia, and removed "sensitive material." Rumor had it that they were so high-speed they couldn't announce their visit. It cost them two helicopters.

Back in our own little part of the operation, yet another war story was brewing. First Platoon had received the order from the company commander to clear and secure the EOD School about one kilometer up the road to the north. Second Lieutenant DeMoss rapidly redistributed the ammunition within his platoon while I directed Lancaster to commandeer two trucks from the motor pool. We split the platoon, putting half on each truck. I volunteered to take the first vehicle but Jim cut me off and said, "No, Clarence, it's my platoon. I'll go first."

"Okay," I replied. "I'll follow in the second truck a couple of hundred meters behind you. If you make contact we'll dismount and flank up one side or the other and eat up any ambushes or blocking positions."

We were both nervous. I threw him a flak jacket that I had found in one of the office buildings. "Here, you might need this." I said grinning. "They always shoot the TC of the first vehicle."

He smiled faintly and shrugged, obviously unamused. Nobody wanted to TC, that is, ride in the front of the vehicle next to the driver. Traditionally the senior man rides up front to navigate and direct the driver. This is great during peacetime training when it's cold and raining and the TC is spared the discomfort inflicted by the elements. Since it *always* rains when we go to the field, senior NCOs and lieutenants often jockey for a TC seat. As I surveyed the trucks, however, I observed that now the place of honor had little appeal, and the men crowded into the backs of the vehicles, where they were protected by the metal sides of the trucks. They oriented their weapons outward.

Before we left, I instructed my driver to pull over for a moment. I sprinted to a large square sewer cover, lifted it, and carried it to the truck. It was extremely heavy and difficult to position between my body and the door. The men in the back roared with laughter. "Hey, XO, what's the matter? Afraid the windshield won't stop a round?"

"Aw, shut your yap," I said jokingly. "Anybody want to trade spots?" Nobody did. I thought to myself, "As the XO in peacetime I always TC, so I guess I have to now." To do otherwise would ruin my credibility, not to mention my chances of getting to TC back at Fort Bragg in the winter . . . assuming I got back.

As we rolled along toward the EOD site, it occurred to me that an enemy ambush anywhere along the route we were presently traveling would be devastating. The jungle was extremely thick, leaving little room for maneuvering. The road was a narrow cut bordered by steep embankments on both sides.

My silent deliberations of the situation ended abruptly when we pulled up to a three-way intersection and dismounted. As we crept along the eastern fork that led into the compound, the fact that everyone was exhausted from the previous attack was evident. The interval between men was too close and they were far from alert as we moved in two columns, one on each side of the road. Some NCOs attempted to whisper corrections, but their instructions had little impact, since the tactical situation did not allow them to speak loudly enough to be heard by many of the men.

Suddenly, an explosion and a scream pierced the air. A man had fallen victim to a booby trap. "I'm hit! . . . I'm hit!" he screamed.

"Medic! Medic!" Someone cried.

For a moment we were so astonished that no one reacted or fired a shot. When we finally went into action and began to move forward to seek cover, we became engaged by enemy fire coming from a guardhouse less than fifty meters away on the left side of the road. The men began to fire at the guardhouse but their shots had little effect, as the terrain prevented any effective fire. Most of the rounds went high.

The man was still screaming hysterically, unnerving the rest of us. I spotted the medic, who was hiding in a hole shuddering with fear. I yelled, "Dammit, Doc, get over there and help him out!" I moved up on the right side as I shouted.

Lieutenant DeMoss was on the left side and I could hear him screaming at the lead squad leader on the right side. "Move up and flank around from the right!" he barked.

When I reached the front, the squad leader was immobilized by shock. The left side was pinned down by enemy fire.

All of a sudden CPL Mark Ruiz, from the lead squad on the left side, dashed forward across open terrain and moved to a berm just in front of the enemy position. His action was undoubtedly similar to those made by heroes of wars past. His team followed him in a chain reaction, moving into a position where they could effectively blast the house. They brought up a .30 caliber machine gun we had taken from the logistics site and riddled the enemy position. Steel and concrete flew everywhere.

An endless minute passed, and we began to inch forward. Suddenly, an M203 gunner froze and glanced down at his feet. I knew by his icy posture that something was wrong. He turned his head slowly, looked me directly in the eye, and pointed to the ground, "Sir, be careful; this whole area is rigged with booby traps."

I looked down and noticed that explosive det cord ran between my legs to the road, where it was wrapped around a 4.2-inch mortar round.

"Oh, NO!!!" I blurted. I heard a chorus of obscenities as everyone began to realize the ugly predicament we had gotten ourselves into. We crept forward, cautiously checking the ground before taking each step. As the booby traps were identified, each man pointed out their exact locations to the next soldier in the column. Sweat poured from our brows under the unbearable strain. I examined every twig and patch of dirt before me, imagining that something was going to explode between my legs at any moment and leave me squirming on the ground with stubs of raw hamburger.

We made it through and cleared the first barracks from a hillside. The tall grenadier took his usual methodical aim, pumping 40mm rounds from his M203 grenade launcher into the windows. With a shotgun slung loosely over his back at a forty-five-degree angle and with bandoleers of ammunition hanging across his shoulders and chest, he would lob a couple of rounds from his M203. Moving in closer, he would blast away with his shotgun, shifting his fire at the last moment as the clearing team assaulted. We cleared the entire complex like this, hammering the buildings from the outside from hasty support positions while part of a squad moved in to clear each structure.

In thirty minutes nearly every building had been cleared except for the enemy arms room. We attempted to breach it with an AT4 but it was too well built. The only solution was to crawl through a window and hand out the weapons and ammunition, loading them on one of the trucks to take back to Cerro Tigre.

The medic finally linked up with the man who had tripped the booby trap. He was not as seriously injured as we had first thought but had taken some shrapnel in the arm and was medevaced out.

While we were emptying the arms room, the sergeant who was pulling left side security began to gesture urgently toward the jungle. Something moved, and he pumped three rounds into a bush, cursing violently at his target. There was much squawking and feathers flew. He had killed a duck. Everyone looked at him accusingly as he shrugged his shoulders and tried not to look embarrassed.

"It didn't sound like a duck!" He protested. "Anybody could have mistakened it. What's a goddamned duck doing here anyway? Shit . . . ain't my fault."

Everyone was on edge, and the fear that permeated the situation magnified the slightest sound or movement. The potential for panic is always present in troops where the threat of physical danger exists. When the injured soldier screamed in agony we almost lost our momentum and self-discipline. Human material is very volatile and the professional officer or NCO must take an unromantic view of man's behavior under stress. Unlike blanks, live ammunition causes disorganization. Men look for cover. Enemy fire comes at them and their thoughts scatter; they no longer think as a group but as individuals. Each man wants to stay put in any sanctuary he can find. The only way they can be brought back into line is with strong leadership, or by an act of courage by men who must expose themselves to the point of suicide so they can inspire their fellows.

Corporal Ruiz was such a man. If he hadn't gotten up and sprinted forward like he did, we might have been brutally punished. Later we had discovered that the booby traps were command-detonated from the guardhouse. Fortunately for the injured man, and for the rest of us, the first booby trap failed to set off the mortar round, giving Ruiz time to suppress the enemy before they could set off any more of the deadly little devices.

We finished loading the truck with the captured weapons and ammunition. Then Lancaster and I and a fire team for security headed back toward Cerro Tigre to link up with the rest of the company, leaving First Platoon to secure the EOD site. By the time we got back, preparations had already begun to defend against an enemy counterattack. The motor pool was full of trucks and forklifts that we hot-wired and used to move 100-pound bags of rice from the mess hall to build and fortify fighting positions.

Although the materials we used to prepare our deliberate perimeter defense were far from conventional, we still adhered to the principles of defending by emplacing crew-served weapons and designating a reaction force. We even stockpiled enemy weapons and ammunition at our own fighting positions in case our remaining basic load was inadequate to do the job. We made Molotov cocktails out of some rum and fertilizer we found in order to augment our claymores and grenades. We would take no chances. A counterattack was probable. The intelligence we had on this place had been wrong. There were more than eighty enemy personnel on the objective when we hit, and we were lucky to have "caught 'em with their pants down." Most of them ran. If they had been more alert or better prepared things could have gotten nasty for us.

The amount and variety of materials and equipment we found at the logistics site stretched the imagination. Tons of communications equipment, and brand-new uniforms still in their boxes, were everywhere. I walked into the installation commander's office and noticed he had as much clothing in his personal wardrobe as was in our entire company supply room.

At Cerro Tigre, American soldiers secure a prisoner of war (*top*) and load him on a truck. After the attack on the EOD school we commandeered this truck (*bottom*) and used it to evacuate enemy weapons, explosives, and POWs. *SPC James Barbour*

We continued to collect PDF soldiers who fled and then turned themselves in to us because they had nowhere to go. We tied them to chairs and blindfolded them. Some of them were just young boys. But they were the enemy.

Later that day we were replaced by a platoon from Alpha Company. Word came down that we had to conduct an attack in Colón that night. The platoon from Alpha Company came in on a CH-47; it took us three separate lifts on the same bird to get back to Fort Sherman. I was on the last lift out for the company so I took time to brief the platoon leader on our defensive plan and showed him around the place. When the last sortie lifted off we flew for forty-five minutes or so, landed and refueled, and then took off and flew to Fort Kobbe. Lieutenant Corrigan and I gave one another a puzzled look. We headed for the pilots in search of an explanation.

"Hey, Chief," I said. "We need to go to Fort Sherman ASAP because we have a mission tonight."

"Sorry," he said, shaking his head, "but we can't fly without our night vision goggles. That's why we came back here . . . so we could get them."

"Well, how long will that take?"

"Don't know for sure."

I was beginning to get upset with him. "Why the hell didn't you think of this before you started flying this mission?" I asked. "How are we supposed to link up with the rest of our company?"

"We weren't told you guys had any mission . . . but I'll see if I can get one of the other birds to fly you." Chief turned and walked toward another aircraft parked on the field.

I yelled after him. "Hey, Chief, can you call Fort Sherman and let 'em know we'll be late?"

"No problem, Sir, I'll be back in a minute."

Temporarily satisfied and at a loss for what to do, Corrigan, an engineer, and I plopped down on the cool grass and tore open an MRE. We munched slowly and stared ahead in silence, too tired to speak. After we had finished eating, we got up and walked over to the other aircraft, where several pilots were talking. One was telling the others about his first combat flight.

"Yeah, Colón is a bloodbath, tracers flying everywhere," he re-counted. "Snipers have already shot down a couple of our choppers. This one unit wanted me to medevac a single wounded guy out. Can you believe that, fly only one guy all the way to Howard Air Force Base. What a waste!"

"Waste of what?" I cut in. Corrigan, the engineer, and I were glaring at him with as much disdain and disrespect as possible.

"Ah . . . mm . . . Oh, nothing actually," he stammered. "I mean . . . since we flew him, no problem."

Another pilot interjected, "Listen to this. I just dropped some captain off on a hot LZ in Colón. The idiot wanted me to wait around while he linked up with his point of contact on the ground. I told him, 'No way, pal,' and got the hell out of there."

"Wow!" said Corrigan. "Who would expect you to wait around under those circumstances?"

I agreed with their reasoning.

We found out later that the "idiot" in the story was Captain Dyer, our commander. But the story the pilots told was incomplete and our commander filled us in on what had actually happened. When he had arrived at Fort Sherman on the first lift from Cerro Tigre, he was ushered onto a helicopter so he could be briefed about our up-and-coming mission in Colón. Nobody told him where he was going, however, or whom he had to link up with to get his orders. The pilots set him down in Colón, and Captain Dyer immediately got in the prone position, faced out, and pulled security. In the darkness he could hear Panamanian voices.

"Man . . . I thought I was surrounded by the enemy!" He recalled. Actually, however, it was only some Panamanian detainees being held by American troops. In the end he received his briefing.

Finally, we managed to procure an aircraft and were headed back to Fort Sherman. The mission was beginning to take its toll on us and fatigue was all-consuming.

When we landed we were told that the mission had been scratched for the night. We were relieved and immediately moved to the billets, where we collapsed into our bunks and slept deeply until the next morning.

III Colón: A City in Chaos

The next morning we began to prepare and refit for Colón. A businesslike atmosphere prevailed, keeping conversation in the barracks to a minimum. The men cleaned and oiled their weapons meticulously, not wishing to gamble on a weapon that wouldn't fire during a critical moment.

That afternoon Captain Dyer took me and the platoon leaders to Colón to take a look at some aerial photos and maps of that city where our objective, DENI headquarters, was located. (DENI is to Panama what the FBI is to the United States.) We drove about twenty kilometers around the southern edge of Limon Bay, passing through the Gatun Locks that split the Canal.

We ran into the roadblock set up by LT Matt Miller from Delta Company and things became momentarily tense. Because we were driving jeeps and not Humvees, Delta did not immediately recognize us nor we them. As we came around the bend in the road, several soldiers had their weapons trained on us. We stopped and Captain Dyer stepped out and walked toward the road block. I adjusted the leaf site on the M203 grenade launcher I was carrying and took up aim, prepared to lob a round on the roadblock. The crisis subsided when the Delta guys recognized Captain Dyer. They waved us through and we proceeded on our way until we arrived at a schoolhouse.

Once there we made sketches of the objective area by copying the aerial photos. Then we returned to Fort Sherman. The commander would fly back to Colón and continue to plan and coordinate with 4-17th, 7th Infantry Division, to whom we would be attached for the operation. Meanwhile, I would move the company by truck along the overland route we had just taken for the reconnaissance. We were to link up at the bottleneck, a narrow strip of land that leads into the city, which covers about three square kilometers surrounded by water.

We convoyed the company to Colón without incident in four five-ton trucks. When we pulled up to the checkpoint just short of the bottleneck, we could hear the crack of sporadic gunfire.

"Jesus Christ!" yelled Crittenden as he grabbed his ruck. "Get off the truck! . . . Get down!"

It didn't take the men long to get off the vehicles and scurry for cover. We linked up with the commander and moved through a field of tall elephant grass, stopping short of the bottleneck on the ruins of an old building. Not long after we had arrived and established a company perimeter, a lieutenant from the 7th Infantry Division linked up with us. He would guide us through the passage point or

Upon receiving a call reporting that one hundred PDF soldiers were holed up in an abandoned bus depot, we went to investigate. Here we're moving out from the ruins of a building just short of the bottleneck leading into Colón. *SPC Lawrence Bateman*

bottleneck, and set up a blocking position while we passed through his platoon to conduct the attack. He informed us that the fighting had been fierce and resulted in the death of several American soldiers on the previous days. I got the impression he was not enthusiastic about going back through the bottleneck again. The 7th ID guys had endured a tough fight there before we arrived.

Bravo Company was part of Team Coggins, named after Major Coggins, 4-17th Battalion XO. Also included in the task organization was B Company 4-17, a vulcan squad, an engineer squad, field artillery battery, C Company 2-27, a Navy SEALs Sniper Team, and a platoon of military police (MPs). All of the units were part of the brigade task force commanded by Colonel Kellogg. While the rest of the battalion conducted an amphibious assault from Coco Solo to the eastern side of Colón, we would infiltrate northward through the bottleneck and attack the DENI headquarters.

Our specific mission was to conduct a deliberate attack on the Cristobal DENI police station, where both PDF and Dignity Battalion troops were reported to be making a last stand. We would then secure the Panama Canal Commission (PCC) control tower in the adjoining wing and the U.S. Consulate across the street. Movement to the objective would be tricky. The PDF were arming the Digbats as well as criminals that had been freed by the PDF commander who wanted to make matters more complicated for us. On order we were to move north and restore law and order along the western edge of the city after the attack had been completed. Evidently, looting was fast becoming a serious problem.

The rules of engagement were plain and simple; "Close with and destroy the enemy." Coordinating instructions with respect to civilians varied slightly, however, and were as follows:

1. Shoot all armed civilians.
2. Looters, if armed, will be killed.
3. Unarmed looters will be dealt with as follows:
   a. Fire a warning shot over their head.
   b. Fire a shot near the person(s).
   c. Shoot to wound.

After coordinating with the platoon leader from 7th ID, we waited for the order to attack. Perimeter security was downgraded to 33 percent to allow the men to rest. Looking around I observed several uniform changes by the men. Most had removed the glint tape from their arms and kept it in their pockets to reduce the likelihood of being shot at because of the reflection caused by the tape. Many also had cut the fingers off their black leather gloves and wore headbands under their kevlar helmets. They did this not because of Rambo movies, but because of practical necessity. Ordinary gloves, though they afford protection, do not permit the fingertip sensitivity required to feel a trigger, selector switch, or volume control on a radio. By cutting off the fingertips on the leather gloves you had both hand protection (an absolute necessity when moving under fire in a MOUT environment) and finger sensitivity. Headbands worn around the forehead keep the sweat from running into your eyes and blinding you. Of course, Army uniform policy frowns upon "Rambo gloves" and headbands, and so did I before Operation Just Cause. It did not take me long, however, to disregard some uniform policies in the face of practical necessity. Enforcement of unit standards is critical, but dogmatic adherence to standards that no longer make sense is questionable.

Another uniform violation that one often sees in peacetime, but which I didn't see in Panama, was the unbuckled LCE vest. If your LCE is unbuckled you cannot IMT (use the Individual Movement Technique) under fire. It gets twisted and caught on everything and bangs around, calling attention to your location. If it is unbuckled you cannot conduct a magazine change very well, and failure to maintain a steady rate of suppressive fire at a critical moment could result in an unpleasant circumstance. Also, an unbuckled LCE swings to and fro, allowing your grenades to batter against everything. Not a very prudent way to move about.

The evening dragged on, interrupted only by the relentless whizzing and awful crack of rounds exploding in the distance. Grimshaw continually updated us on the big picture as he faithfully monitored the radio. Again, however, the mission was canceled for several reasons, including lack of A-C130 support and problems with the rest of the battalion.

The next day we called 4-17th for resupply. Most of us had not eaten since we left Fort Sherman. In the meantime, the commander, platoon leaders and I decided to move north to the 7th ID platoons headquarters less than one hundred meters up the bottleneck. At least we could get water from them. We called ahead and moved to the building. It was four stories high. When we reached the top a Navy SEAL Team was set up with a .50 caliber sniper system and 7.62 bolt-action rifle. They had a spotting scope as well, and were casually picking off armed civilians in accordance with the rules of engagement. Although, how you "shoot to wound" with a .50 caliber sniper rifle still baffles me.

We were well into the morning when we received a call from the MPs back at the detrucking point where we had first dismounted. They said that more than one hundred PDF soldiers were holed up in an abandoned bus depot just to the south of the bottleneck. Moving as quickly as possible to the scene, we immediately surrounded the building. The MPs used a loudspeaker mounted on a Humvee and did the typical "come out with your hands up" number. It didn't work. Results were minimal. Second and Third platoons sealed off the area while First Platoon went in with the commander to clear the building.

Everything was going smoothly until we heard a scream over the radio. Two men were clearing a room utilizing the high-low technique. Each occupied the side of a doorway leading into a room. When the first man busted the door open, the second turned the corner, his weapon off safe and ready to fire into the room. Unfortunately, the shotgun accidentally discharged as he turned the corner, blowing away the other man's knee. The injured soldier was medevaced out, but he will never fully recover. From then onward, muzzle control became a priority. Peacetime breeds bad habits, like carelessly waving your weapon around. But after that incident, the men got on anyone who failed to control his weapon. We all were sorry for the man who was injured. He was one of many good soldiers who made a sacrifice to get the job done.

Western movies and police shows often present a misleading depiction of battle injuries. The good guy gets shot but keeps on going—a couple of bandages and a little rest and he's ready for the next scene.

The reality, however, is much uglier. When burning steel penetrates flesh and bone, it can cause irreparable damage that a man may never fully recover from. One of our guys caught an AK47 round through his calf. It did not look bad at the time and he was rather calm, not making a big fuss over his injury. We found out later that his calf bone had been completely shattered, probably past the point of resetting.

When First Platoon emerged, Third rotated in to clear the next wing of the bus depot. I accompanied them. A terrible stench overwhelmed us as we entered the building, and we quickly forgot our nervousness. The ground floor had been used by the locals as a public latrine and was covered by human feces and garbage. The odor caused the man ascending below me on the stairwell to wretch. My own stomach began to protest what my eyes and nose were experiencing. One of the men glared at me when we reached the top floor.

"How can people live like this?" he rasped in a tone edged with disgust.

"Hell," countered SSG James Popp, Third Platoon sergeant, sarcastically. "At least they use the first floor mostly. They can't be all that bad."

It was true; most of the defecation was confined to the first floor and evidence of an unwritten agreement among the locals to use the bus depot as a public latrine was obvious. It was the only building in the area like it. Apparently, running water had not been available for some time, resulting in a makeshift solution that at least restricted the unsanitary conditions to a centralized location.

Ten prisoners were captured by the time we had finished. We left them with the MPs and moved back to our company perimeter, waiting for the word to attack. Glad for the temporary reprieve from hostile activities, we hunkered down in the sparse shade of a small grove of trees. Resupply now arrived on a regular basis, and Staff Sergeant Lancaster looked scornfully at some of the headquarters fellows.

"Get your goat-smelling asses up out of them gopher holes and come with me to get the chow!" he ordered.

One of the men rolled over and moaned, tearfully complaining.

Soldiers wait outside the bus depot that had been used as a public latrine. No one wanted to enter the building because of the stench. *SPC James Barbour*

"But Sergeant Lancaster, my feet are blistered and my head aches. I don't think I'm up to any heavy lifting."

"Aw, shit," retorted Lancaster, puffing fiercely on a cigarette. "I suppose we'll just have to leave you back here when we move out so . . ."

Varoom! Varoom! Rockets spewed from the Cobra as it banked and came back around for another pass on the DENI building just over the horizon. The PDF had made the fatal error of sniping at a Cobra.

Varoom! Varoom! The sky filled with fire and smoke, obscuring the building in a black cloud.

"Now ain't that the damndest thing!" exclaimed Lancaster. Chow was momentarily forgotten. All of us were glued to the spectacle of a Cobra gunship dumping its deadly ordnance on some stubborn pocket of resistance.

Not five minutes afterward, white flags waved desperately out of the windows of the building. Reports came in that some of the PDF had surrendered. Some still remained, however. We were very pleased that a Cobra would be on station for our attack. There's nothing like high-tech to get you through the tough times. Dusk came quickly and we readied ourselves.

We moved to the base of the 7th ID platoon headquarters, which blocked the bottleneck, and dropped off our rucksacks. They would be brought to us after we secured the DENI Headquarters. An ominous silence filled the air as men silently clasped one another's hands and wished each other good luck. This reflected the bonding that had developed among the men. It is clearly fixed in my mind and I shall never forget it.

The commander waved me over to him. He cocked an eyebrow and said slowly, "We are going to use the 105mm cannons in a direct-fire mode. They will pull up on the southern corner of the objective with an MP escort. That's where we think most of the enemy are. They will fire eighteen rounds at point-blank range while we wait in an assault position just to the southeast. When they're done, Second and First Platoons will assault the building supported by Third. Once in the building, Third will face outward and provide security."

"How close did you say we would be to the 105mm cannon rounds?" I asked hesitantly.

"Probably not more than thirty meters, with a two-story building separating us from the blast."

I blinked and swallowed, not really believing what I was hearing. Crittenden, who was listening to our conversation, mused, "Well, I guess we got us a new definition of danger close, huh? Why, range control would never let us get away with this kind of stuff on a live-fire training exercise back home."

The sun was sliding below the horizon when we began moving through the bottleneck. The narrow strip of earth and concrete was used as a temporary storage area for products transported by the great commercial ships that used Colón as a port of call. Many of the connexes had been busted open by looters. Clothing, shoes, and liquor were scattered everywhere.

Total stealth characterized our movement. The company column wrapped in and around the connexes as we moved forward through the maze. The floodlights were annoying and we stuck to the comfort of the dark shadows that provided a sense of security from enemy observation. I felt like one sneaky bandit among many sneaky bandits.

The unit's tempo increased as we drew near the objective. Hearts pounded and breath quickened as our adrenalin began to flow, supercharging our senses. We were in a state of hyperconsciousness again, sensing the world around us in slow motion. The mindset of the soldier on the battlefield is highly disturbed, but it ensures comprehension and the ability to react quickly to a volatile environment.

I passed by Third Platoon, which dropped off to establish a support position. I could hear Captain Dyer cussing vehemently as he grabbed a soldier and thrust him toward the assault position. A couple of confused men caused the entire column to stall momentarily. We moved in to find a position, pressing against the ground and the side of the building that separated us from the 105mm cannons.

The roar of the first round was deafening, so loud that it didn't register as sound. I couldn't hear anything but instead experienced a sensation like being smashed on the head by a baseball bat. The sensation started at my head and reverberated all the way down to my toes, ending in an uncontrollable shudder. It was impossible to distinguish between the cannon firing and the rounds impacting on the building, since the two explosions were so close. Shock waves followed the blasts, causing a bat to fall from a tree and crawl up the sleeve of the commander's radio-telephone operator. He forgot the battle and screamed for Chris Bennett to pull the bat out of his sleeve. It all happened in slow motion.

"My God, it's a bat! A bat is crawling up my arm!" the man shouted. "Pull it out! Pull it out!"

"Shit, I got other things to worry about," Bennett replied in a matter-of-fact tone that seemed out of place.

Burning shrapnel and chunks of concrete rained down on us. The enemy AK47 fire that shot back from the building was quickly silenced by the cannons. A squad from Third Platoon was caught in the cross fire. The MPs, who had been told explicitly not to fire until they withdrew and then only if absolutely necessary, were shooting at us. Lieutenant Corrigan ran out to pull his squad back, only to get pinned down himself. The crack of AT4s and LAWs split the air, causing great damage to the buildings.

"Let's go!" somebody shouted.

The firing stopped. We sprinted to the breach, rounds firing overhead, and ran into the building. As we entered, I looked at the commander and Grimshaw and pointed to the left down the hallway. "Hey, has anybody cleared that room?" I asked.

"I don't know," replied Captain Dyer. We moved into room-clearing formation. I crouched. "You go low and I'll go high!" screamed the commander.

"I've already decided that!" I replied. We burst into the room wild-eyed and intense.

"All clear!"

"Roger, lets move upstairs!"

"Okay, friendlies coming out!" We yelled as we exited the room.

Upstairs, we moved along a concrete balcony about three feet high and twelve inches thick. The rest of the upper floor was open. Suddenly, automatic fire whizzed by our heads and splattered the wall behind us.

"What in the . . . ! Who the hell is that?" Grimshaw screamed. I heard someone yell, "Sniper!"

"No way," I said. "Snipers don't fire an automatic!" I removed my helmet, placed it on the muzzle of my weapon, and poked it above the balcony wall.

"Grimshaw!" I shouted. "See where the fire is coming from when they shoot at my helmet."

"Hell no, Sir," he replied. "I know where it's coming from. It's coming from out there and we're in here!" The room erupted into hysterical laughter.

"I guess you're right," I conceded. "That's all we really need to know."

Broken glass and rubbled concrete tore at us as we crawled on the floor. When the building was finally clear, the commander told me to go outside and begin the consolidation and reorganization phase. He took Second Platoon to secure the PCC portion of the building.

Outside, Second Platoon linked up with the rest of the company, which was marching a captured POW at gunpoint. The commotion had died down. An A-C130 was flying overhead, conducting a ground search for us. We all gathered in our command post on the stairs of an American missionary's house adjacent to the DENI building.

"This shit is beginning to grate on my nerves," complained Lancaster. "How long is this friggin' war gonna last? I got a court appearance coming up."

"That's the least of your worries," countered our company FIST.

"This is all becoming sort of surrealistic," remarked the commander. "I expect to wake up at any moment."

Abruptly, Lieutenant Corrigan and the second lieutenant from the 7th ID came around the corner and joined our group. "Hey, Sir, those MP son-of-a-bitches were shooting at us!" Corrigan told Captain Dyer. "They almost killed us. They shot at you too while you were in the building!"

"Yeah," said the 7th ID lieutenant. "They shot at us in the bottleneck. A couple of days ago they were behind us on an attack and two of my guys were hit, one killed."

"They weren't supposed to fire," said Captain Dyer. "We went over the plan three times with them!"

Crittenden waved a big hand. "Those shitheads just want to fire their weapons and be heroes. They need to mind their own business and stick to issuing traffic tickets."

The commander was fuming. He spun around and said, "Let's go find the MPs. I want to talk to that lieutenant."

The matter was solved after a heated discussion in which Major Coggins, 4-17th Battalion XO, saved the MP lieutenant from a fate far worse than the verbal reprimand he received.

When it appeared that things were quieting down, our company FIST began telling us about the missionaries. "I had a long talk with them while you guys were clearing the DENI building. Their next door neighbors are supposedly real friendly with the PDF."

"Oh really?" asked Captain Dyer. "Maybe we should check it out."

We moved around the side of the building where the couple lived. A woman appeared when we knocked on the door. We told her she must get out of the house while we searched it. She came out, followed by three men.

"Wait a minute," I said. "I thought the missionary said a couple lived here, not a whole commune."

The couple huddled together, staring at us with fearful eyes. The other two characters tried to appear innocent as they gently stroked and cuddled some puppies that we had also pulled out of the apartment.

"Tricky bastards," said Lancaster. "Look at 'em, trying to look like members of the Humane Society."

As we searched the apartment, the husband became nervous and spilled the beans on the other two. Yes, they were Dignity Battalion members.

"Bingo!"

We proceeded to search, silence, and segregate the prisoners. Sergeant First Class Perez interrogated them and found out that when they knew we were about to attack, their commander had told them to put on civilian clothes and run for it. He also released criminals throughout the city and equipped them with weapons to further thwart us. After processing the POWs we went to 50 percent security.

I had just settled down when the radio crackled. It was Staff Sergeant Popp calling me.

"Bravo 5, this is Bravo 3-5, over."

"Go ahead 3-5."

"Roger. We got a man approaching our perimeter with something in his hand, over."

"Bravo 3-5, this is Bravo 5. Fire a warning shot first, then shoot to wound."

"This is Bravo 3-5, Wilco . . . Out!"

Unfortunately, the man did not heed the warning shot and continued to move toward us. When he was seventy-five or one hundred meters away, Staff Sergeant Popp took aim to wound, but the lighting in the street was poor. He shot the man through the rib cage. The man fell, attempted to clamber back up a street lamp, and slumped back to the ground. Closer inspection revealed that the man was carrying a bottle of liquor. Evidently he was so drunk that not even the warning shots could sober him up. He was bleeding profusely from the back of his rib cage where the round had exited his body and created a hole the size of a softball. The blood reeked of booze. The men carried the body to the CP and dropped it off next to First Sergeant Butler, who was sleeping at the time. When Butler woke up a little later he was not happy to discover that he had unknowingly rolled up against a dead man. He almost cursed.

In the solitude of the night, I began to wonder what made men submit themselves to the ordeal of battle again and again. This was our fourth engagement and it was not getting any easier. One thing is for certain, noble men will not disgrace themselves in front of other men, whose respect they need for their own self-respect. I was surrounded by men whose training, self-respect, and loyalty to their fellows overcame any physical terror or desperate desire not to die.

"Yes," I thought. "These are some fine men, and I am indeed fortunate to have kept company with them."

Fear is an uncomfortable sensation. It is not merely a state of mind but a physical affliction manifesting itself through hyperventilation, trembling, and loss of bowel control. It has one of two effects. It either prompts men to do the correct thing and fight like they have been trained, or it causes a unit to falter. Strong leadership at the decisive place and time is the determining factor. Leadership is the backbone of unit morale.

Unit morale is not necessarily linked to the number or proportion of deaths the unit suffers, but is contingent on the duration of the men's exposure to combat. Large battles that occurred prior to the late nineteenth century often ended with 40 to 50 percent of the soldiers dead or wounded on any given day. The prospect of death for

Members of Delta Company hold up a Panamanian flag at sunrise the morning after D-Day at Madden Dam. Victory was at hand. *LT Eric Edin*

an infantryman who fought a couple of battles a year was great. Combat was seasonal then, however, and soldiers spent most of the year in the fields or inside, making the situation more bearable. During World Wars I and II the casualty rate was somewhat lower than in other wars in history, but it was still very high. Soldiers were "in it" for the duration, and this realization produced a sense of despair that can be linked to the high casualty rate. In contrast, only about one in fifty U.S. soldiers who served in Vietnam was killed. Episodes of intense combat were for the most part restricted to frontline units. The lower death rate in Vietnam was counterbalanced by a high wounded ratio due to a superb American helicopter medevac system that left more veterans maimed and crippled than dead. Nevertheless, men had the opportunity to rotate out of a combat zone after pulling a tour.

A study by the U.S. Army concluded that during World War II, an average soldier would break down after 200 to 240 days in combat. Similar studies conducted worldwide have reached the same conclusion. This certainly varies across nations and between individuals in varying combat environments. The point is, however, that the lethality of weapons has increased a million-fold since the nineteenth century, yet it is physically safer to be a soldier today than it was then. The problem now is that battles can continue for weeks, months, and years, slowly grinding men into fearful submission.

The key to preparing men to deal with the rigors of combat is training, not patriotic rhetoric. Rhetoric is virtually irrelevant as far as actual soldiering is concerned. Sure, soldiers are human beings with loyalties, and many feel better if they have ideological justification for what they do. But soldiers can be made to fight and die as bravely for Allah as they can for God, Mom, and apple pie. Politicians and priests send soldiers to fight for political and ideological reasons. The grunt fights for more basic motives, and abstract theories, policies, and concepts are replaced by immediate objectives, intense personal loyalties, and the desire to survive.

A unique bond of trust between soldiers begins to form during rigorous training in peacetime. The cohesion that starts when soldiers are tired, hungry, wet, and miserable during training intensifies under the fear of combat. You depend on the man next to you for your life just as he depends on you. If either one of you fails and lets the other down, you could easily be maimed or killed. If your fellow soldier is technically incompetent, poorly trained, or physically weak, he is a threat to you and the unit. Men like this are necessarily despised and often ostracized in an attempt to force them to correct their shortcomings. For the modern battlefield, more and more emphasis is placed on small-unit dynamics, where individual soldiers and leaders must show more initiative and skill than ever before, often operating independently in small teams and squads. Thus, a small group of men must rely utterly on themselves and the skills they have developed in peacetime in order to be successful and survive. Karl von Clausewitz asserted in *On War* that an army that maintains its cohesion and discipline under the harshest circumstances in both victory and defeat is imbued with "true military spirit" that can only be attained through sheer determination and experiencing privation during training.

Contrary to the beliefs of some ivory-tower thinkers, the warrior ethic is not an illusion, nor is it a consequence of brainwashing in which soldiers do not know what they are really doing. Soldiers are very aware of what they are doing, and if they are well trained, they take every possible measure to succeed and survive.

The attack on the DENI headquarters was the last time we had to "close with and destroy the enemy." The rules of engagement were about to change again and would place demands on us that we had never encountered in basic infantry training.

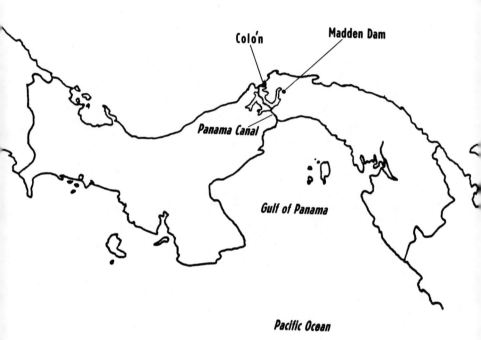

Caribbean

Colón   Madden Dam

Panama Canal

Gulf of Panama

Pacific Ocean

Constables

Ask Questions First, Shoot Later

Rays of sunlight crept over the horizon, casting long shadows across the wet dew-covered grass in front of the DENI head-quarters. It was December 23rd, two days before Christmas, and here we were in the tropical port of Colón—right out of a chapter from Joseph Conrad. Our next mission was to move north along the western seaboard and conduct clearing operations. Then we were to designate platoon sectors and begin patrolling to establish law and order.

Colón, once a busy and prosperous city that teemed with activity, was now in a shambles. This was the city that shipped over $4 billion of merchandise in and out of the Free Zone each year. The port city handles over two million tons of cargo annually, under the flags of 15,000 ships from sixty or so different nations. Usually, ships sailed regularly into Cristóbal Harbor when beginning or ending a Canal transit, but the shipping lanes were motionless this day, and an eerie silence hung in the air. The narrow strip of land, or choke point, that served as a temporary storage area for cargo, had been ravaged by looters. Connexes had been burst open, their contents spilled across the asphalt pavement. Smashed store and house windows and mer-chandise and debris scattered throughout the streets provided the backdrop for yet another episode in our Central American excursion. This time our mission was to establish law and order.

The role of police officer or constable is a difficult one for an unbridled warrior still fresh from the fight to assume. High-strung and chomping at the bit, we would soon be forced to suppress our aggression and adopt a more civil approach to dealing with our surroundings. Tension ran high as we moved north toward the Hotel Washington, where we would establish our company command post. Before we could do that, however, we would have to show the local population that we were a large enough element to be formidable.

The streets came alive as people appeared from every door and window, cheering us like liberators. Moving at the rear of the column I overheard a conversation between SSG Joseph Moore, a squad leader from Third Platoon, and Staff Seargeant Popp.

"An invasion force hell," laughed Staff Sergeant Popp. "These people love us." And they did.

"Yeah, just like when the 82nd marched through France during the second World War," Moore snickered. "Vive Bush!"

"You sure that happened in World War II?" asked Popp.

"Of course it did. Don't you know nothing about 82nd history?"

"Oh, now I remember," recalled Popp. "That's right, that's when all them guys got to pick and choose any woman they wanted. I seen it in a movie. By the looks of some of these babes hanging themselves out the windows, we should do just as well. Hey, take a look at that one," he whistled. "I can tell she's interested just by the way she's ignoring me."

Both men laughed halfheartedly but kept a wary eye on the locals, suspiciously turning their heads and pointing their weapons at any odd sounds or metallic glints of light. We did in fact feel like liberators as we marched through the slums of Colón. The scene, however, did not do much for the senses. The stench created by the garbage and human feces in the streets was unbearable. Slime trickled down from the upper stories of buildings and dribbled down our faces and necks, as we were forced to constantly observe for any threat from above.

"Goddamn it!" a rifleman cursed as he wiped his freckled forehead. "I didn't join the Army for this bullshit." His buddies nimbly danced out of the way as a glob of slop rained on the spot where they had just been standing. Everyone giggled. Just then two Panamanian men erupted into a conversation and began gesturing for us to follow them down an alley.

"I wouldn't trust them miserable sons of bitches," growled Lancaster as he ran across the street to join us.

"Looks like a trap."

But it wasn't a trap. The two men revealed several weapons that had been cached on an awning over a doorway. Time and time again the locals led us to weapons caches, more than happy to rid themselves of a potential danger. We became the only source of order in a lawless town.

For the time being we inherited the chore of maintaining the peace, searching out PDF and Dignity Battalion members, arresting drunkards, stopping looters, and settling domestic disputes. The collapse of the PDF created a power vacuum that deprived the country of its most stabilizing force and internal security mechanism. The result was widespread anarchy and lawlessness.

The three interrelated concepts of the international Laws of Land Warfare—military necessity, proportionality, and the avoidance of unnecessary suffering—took on a new meaning when applied to the role of the constable. Deadly force could only be used in self-defense and to protect American and Panamanian lives. Minimum force would be used in establishing law and order. Warning shots had to be fired in all cases, and it was mandatory to shoot only to wound. Chambering a round while not in imminent danger and clearing buildings by fire were forbidden. At roadblocks we could fire only if a vehicle attempted to breach, and then we could shoot only to disable the vehicle, not at the occupants.

We scrubbed our faces clean of camouflage to avoid intimidating the locals.

Clearly, the problems that were immediately visible were just the symptoms of a deeper underlying national affliction. Panama, once a vibrant nation of commerce, was now stricken with poverty, U.S. economic sanctions, 20-percent unemployment, and a government riddled with corrupt officials. It was quite apparent that once order was restored, the new government of Guillermo Endara, who had been elected president in May 1989 but kept out of power by Noriega, would have the enormous task of rebuilding a nation whose economy was in a shambles.

Through some not so fortuitous circumstances we found ourselves at the plush and gracious Hotel Washington. Initially, we had set up a perimeter on the outside while the last of the 7th ID soldiers who had occupied the hotel since D-Day vacated the premises. The enormous concrete building with sculpted stone and marble columns was a stark contrast to the red-light district that lay just beyond its outer walls. It was a symbol of wealth and luxury in a land of poverty. Three gates that faced to the south were the only conduit between the elegant courtyard and the garbage-strewn streets of Colón. On the northern side a stone pavilion stretched to a rock wall that held back the turbulent waters of the ocean below. A swimming pool, health spa,

This photo of the entrance to the Hotel Washington was taken from one of
the security positions on the roof while facing south toward the slums of Colón.
PFC David Grimshaw

and outdoor café provided the hotel's guests with every convenience as they enjoyed the view. To the east lay an upper-class neighborhood where Manuel Noriega was said to have a vacation cottage.

When I walked through the front gate into the courtyard I noticed a tall, dark-skinned Panamanian prisoner who had been handcuffed and left in our custody by the 7th ID. He was barefoot and shirtless. Closer examination revealed a battered and bloody face with swollen lips and a closed eye. He babbled away at some unseen menace.

"What's up, Sir?" I asked the commander as I approached the scene. The radio crackled and Captain Dyer became involved in a conversation with the battalion commander.

Grimshaw, noticing my curiosity, responded, "I think he got beat up, Sir."

"No shit." I said. "Who did it and why?"

"I dunno. He was looting or something."

The guy was sweating like a pig and began crying like a child throwing a temper tantrum.

"Well," chuckled Lancaster. "At least we know why he got beat up. I think he's on drugs or something. They found him hiding in the hotel."

Since we would be occupying the hotel I suggested to Sergeant First Class Crittenden that he and I go inside and recon the interior. The NCO scratched his head as a sly grin spread across his face.

"Ah yes, Sir, I think you might be right. We need to find the rooms most suitable for the headquarters—you know, them big ones with all the fancy furniture. Shit, I bet there is even a bar and casino in that joint. Of course, we'll have to put that off limits, Sir," he said with a wink.

As usual, Crittenden's analysis was correct, and we soon found ourselves sitting around the bar drinking orange pop donated by a hotel employee and watching the news on a big screen television that was suspended above the dance floor. The news announcer described the American operation in detail. An Army public affairs officer rattled off some battle statistics and speculated on probable courses of action by the enemy and how the U.S. would handle the situation. He said that some of the PDF might take to the jungles, and we would have to go after them and rout them out. It appeared that we would be at this for an extended period of time. Our attention focused back to our present surroundings.

"Oh if only I could fill my glass with something besides this carbonated sugar water," lamented Lancaster, who had joined us. "Can't drink, can't even fight anymore. . . . That's enough to drive a man to religion! These are hard times."

Crittenden leaned over, playing the part of the sympathetic bartender. "Yeah, ya know, but the thing of it is we can't be losing our wits and gettin' stupid around here. I'll just wait till we get back before I guzzle a cold one."

Lancaster got up and stomped out of the room, grumbling about hard times while the rest of the men who had gathered slumped over the bar and stared into their soda pop, deep in thought. Their camouflage uniforms and rugged equipment made a striking contrast with the elegant background of the bar and casino. As patrons, we looked like we belonged in an old western saloon, not in a modern-day discotheque.

Our reverie was interrupted by a commotion upstairs. We scrambled for our weapons as we slid off the bar stools and headed for the door.

"They went up there! They went up there!" shouted several men who were gathered below a hole in the ceiling. As I approached, I saw SGT Robert Gruber's legs disappear from view as he climbed up into the hole.

"Somebody hand me a pistol," he demanded as he stretched his hand downward. Some of the guys had seen two men with weapons climb into the crawl space between the second and third floors.

"Spread out!" cried Gruber. "I think they're gonna try and punch a hole through the ceiling tiles and get out through one of the rooms." Within minutes we had both the second and third floors covered and were checking the rooms.

"This one's locked!" cried an M60 machine gunner from Third Platoon, pointing toward a door. Blam! Blam! Blam! The door burst open and two of the men cleared it. Empty!

I ran to the stairway where Crittenden was talking to Gruber through a small sliding door that was normally used by repairmen to access the crawl space. The big man couldn't compress his body through the opening.

"Is he alone?" I panted as I ran up to him.

"Yeah," replied Crittenden.

"Here, hold my gear," I told Crittenden as I stripped off my equipment and pulled out my 9mm pistol. The door was just large enough for me to squeeze through. I entered the three-foot-high crawl space into darkness. As my eyes began to adjust I could see a maze of pipes and wires. Footing was treacherous since wooden cross beams spaced about eighteen inches apart were all that would support a man.

"Sergeant Gruber?" I whispered.

"I'm over here, Sir," he replied. "I think they may be in that corner over there."

Not ten feet from where I was I could barely make out Sergeant Gruber pointing to the far corner. As my eyes adjusted to the dimness I gradually became aware that the crawl space was huge, stretching the entire length of the building.

"Sir, I'll move ahead of you," Sergeant Gruber said. "Give me some distance and then follow and cover me."

"Oh God," I thought. "I hope there is nobody in that corner aiming an automatic weapon at us." We moved awkwardly. Sergeant Gruber flicked his flashlight on and off to guide us, holding it as far away from his body as possible to avoid drawing pinpoint fire. There was no way to conceal our approach. Every sound we made echoed in the darkness.

"Those pricks," said Gruber, psyching himself up. "They're not gonna kill me." I tensed in apprehension, sweat running into my eyes.

"Let's recon by fire," I suddenly urged him.

"Okay. Shit, it's not like they don't know we're here," he whispered back. I heard his weapon click off safe as I gripped mine.

We fired. Blam! Blam! Blam! The explosion ripped through the crawl space, echoing off the walls of the confined area. I thought I had ruptured an eardrum. We moved to the corner and discovered that a hole had been punched through a ceiling tile and led into a room. Although disappointed we missed them, I breathed a sigh of relief.

"Coming down!" Gruber yelled as we lowered ourselves into the room. Whoever it was that our men had seen had made good their escape. We stood there looking at one another, soaked in sweat and grinning.

"Sergeant Gruber, you got a set of steel balls," I said.

"Shit, Sir, that's what the Army pays me for." We laughed.

Meanwhile, the hunt for Noriega, who had evaded American attempts to capture him, was underway. Reported sightings of the culprit were abundant. An old woman appeared at the front gate of the hotel, pointing a crooked finger and raving that Noriega had a secret tunnel under the hotel that he had used for an escape route upon the 7th ID's arrival. We were skeptical at first, but an onslaught of corroborating accounts from the locals prompted us to investigate. A quick search of the hotel's basement quickly dismissed the notion of a secret tunnel.

We were also warned that the remnants of the PDF and Dignity Battalions would soon rally and attack us at the hotel. Not wishing to tempt fate, we worked diligently to fortify the hotel.

The company CP was located on the northwest wing of the second floor. We selected that spot because the balcony overlooked the ocean, which we thought to be the least likely avenue of approach. Antenna wires from the hotel's many television sets were used to connect AN PRC 77 radios to the 292 antenna we had emplaced on the rooftop to maximize our FM range. While we were working, a soldier wobbled into the room under the pretense of offering his assistance. Despite the fatigue that clouded my thinking, I knew immediately that he was drunk.

"Hey, you guys want some help with that or . . . or what . . . huh . . .?" he babbled incoherently, his eyes glossy and red.

Captain Dyer looked sharply at him then shifted his attention to me, silently indicating that the man was intoxicated. The room became uncomfortably silent. The intoxicated soldier began throwing equipment and wire around the room, trying to help.

"Don't worry, I'll square this shit away," he drawled. "Yep, no problem." Then he stumbled out of the room just as abruptly as he had entered.

"Secure that son of a bitch! NOW!" demanded the commander, his voice rising in anger. "Where is his weapon?"

Blam! Blam!

"Hey!" cried Grimshaw. "That's coming from the top floor." We sprinted up the stairs to the room where the shots came from. Several of the guys were standing around pointing.

"He went in there," someone said. "He's not making any sense . . . Something about enemy in the neighborhood next to us."

Carefully entering the room, we saw the intoxicated man leaning over the balcony, aiming his M16A2 at some imaginary threat. His head jerked around when he heard us behind him, his eyes wild with intoxication. "Oh no," I thought. "This could get real ugly."

"You fucking shithead," yelled Crittenden as he plowed into the room. "Are you outta your goddamned mind? Who the hell do you think you are anyway?" A tide of blind hatred welled up in the drunk soldier's eyes as he defiantly glared back at the big man.

"You ain't shit, Sarge. Nothin' but a dumb ol' Ranger," he slurred, setting his weapon down as he gathered himself for an assault. "Why I got a good mind to kick your . . ."

Crack! Crittenden's fist crashed against his jaw, knocking the smaller man against the concrete wall.

"What you say? You want some more of this?" roared Crittenden as he closed his hand over the man's throat and repeatedly banged his head on the wall. The rest of us grabbed the two, pulling them apart before Crittenden could beat him so badly that we would have to medevac him.

I nodded to two of the other NCOs. "Confine him to his room," I told them. "Hell, tie the bastard down until he sleeps it off."

Captain Dyer surveyed the scene and stated coldly, "The next man who so much as takes a sip of alcohol while we are here will be court-martialed. XO!"

"Yes, Sir," I replied.

"From now on the bar and casino are off limits. Rotate a guard on it, or whatever you have to do. We need to nip this in the bud before it gets out of hand."

"Airborne, Sir! I'll get on it right away."

The drunk soldier had set a dangerous precedent. The appearance of victory served as an invitation for relaxation, lulling the men into a false sense of security. His behavior was not an isolated case. Our information conduit to the outside and our logistical connection to the rest of the battalion was maintained by CPT Steven Hagan and LT Don Brown, who, in addition to bringing us beans and bullets from Fort Sherman every day, kept us informed on what everybody else was doing. They related numerous security problems involving soldiers that were similar to ours.

One such unfortunate incident occurred at the Madden Dam site, where Delta Company had established a roadblock and checkpoint for all traffic moving north or south. Several days passed without incident at the roadblock, but then one day when two NCOs told the occupants of a vehicle to get out, they spotted a CS (tear gas) grenade in the front seat. The five enemy were immediately forced to lie face down on the road. It was too late. One reached into his shirt and pulled the pin on a grenade. All hell broke loose. When the shooting subsided, nine Americans had been wounded, four very seriously, and all the vehicle's occupants were presumed dead. Afterward, one of the enemy soldiers allegedly moved, and a senior NCO from Delta Company reacted by shooting. The NCO was later accused of murder. But, according to him and others at the scene, he had reacted to a seemingly threatening move by the downed enemy, who had appeared to be reaching for another grenade. This incident was another example of the confusion that arises on the battlefield when soldiers are confronted with a potentially violent threat.

The Delta Company commander reflected on the incident: "When he pulled that pin, we opened up with everything we had. Lucky for us we didn't kill our own guys. We really didn't believe anything like this would happen here that long after H-Hour."

Suspecting that this could be the tip of something much larger, the company commander requested air support. The Cobra gunship flew several dry gun runs. This action failed to have the desired psychological effect, however, due to the less-than-courageous attitude of the Cobra pilot, who refused to fly any lower than 2500 feet. He said he "did not want to jeopardize the safety of his aircraft!"

The commander abruptly responded to the pilot, "Get the hell out of here then. If all you're gonna do is fly around at 2500 feet, I don't need you!"

Not long afterward another unfortunate incident occurred at Madden Dam. A suspicious looking vehicle pulled up to the Delta Company roadblock. The occupants were opening and closing the doors as the vehicle inched forward. An MP vehicle was dispatched to investigate. As the MP pulled up, he attempted to utilize his GTA or Spanish-English translation card and yelled in Spanish. He thought he was saying, "Stop, come here!" but he had actually said, "Go away." After the MP had said this several times, the driver of the vehicle hastily attempted to turn around and speed away. He wasn't quick enough, however, and gunfire shattered the windows of the automobile, killing all the occupants. A perfect example of how the language barrier can be dangerous.

Delta Company personnel became the subject of three separate investigations during the operation at Madden Dam. Interpretation of what is and what is not a war crime is a difficult task. Ambiguity plagued those involved, and interpretation of events varied according to where you were when the alleged event occurred. Interpretation of whether an act was a heroic deed, an unfortunate incident, or an ugly crime also varied with the particular rules of engagement that were in effect at the time and with where the event occurred.

The constable role was the fourth set of rules under which our soldiers found themselves operating in a span of several days. This is testimony to the rapidity of change on the battlefield in Panama, and the transition from one set of rules to the next caused difficult problems for the grunt on the ground. Testimonies too numerous to list here focus on the same problem—"I wasn't sure when to use force, or when I could shoot, or what to do IF . . ."

My colleagues and I suggested on more than one occasion that current infantry training needed to be amended to include distinct modules dealing with rules of engagement. This is not to say that we should forget everything we've ever learned and restrict our training to that based solely on the experience in Panama. We have ample historical antecedents that warn against such a foolhardy shift in doctrine. But we do need to take a hard look at our current doctrine and see if it covers all the contingencies that we may have to deal with in the near future. Overall, American soldiers showed a great deal of restraint and adaptability in Panama. Nevertheless, under the rules of engagement that were unfamiliar to the typical grunt, there were some glaring instances of shortcomings.

After hearing a number of horror stories about lapses in security and the resulting consequences, we tightened up our own show considerably. We broke the company sector down into three platoon sectors with Third to the north, First in the center, and Second to the south. The entire sector was about 1500 meters long and 300 meters wide, with the 7th ID on our eastern boundary. Headquarters and attachments were responsible for the defense of the hotel. The platoons left their M60 machine guns at the hotel, so we had 360 degrees of interlocking fire with crew-served weapons. Under the rules of engagement in effect at the time, the M60s were impractical for patrolling the streets, since they make pinpoint fire difficult and present a threat to innocent bystanders during a firefight. Each platoon had one squad out patrolling its sector at all times, one resting, and one providing local security for the platoon CP. Control measures were established to ensure mutual support and reinforcement between the platoons.

That afternoon, Grimshaw took a frantic call from First Platoon.

"Sir," he said to Captain Dyer as he spun around in his chair. "First has got some PDF trapped in a building, but it's in 7th ID sector!"

"What! Did they coordinate to cross the boundary?" the commander asked.

"Yes, Sir, they said they did."

"Okay. First Sergeant, XO, let's go see what's going on," Captain Dyer instructed.

We gathered up a small party and headed to the location that First had reported. By the time we arrived, a crowd of three or four hundred people had gathered around the scene. Three men, bound and gagged, lay face down on the sidewalk under the watchful eyes of several of our men. Everyone else's attention was riveted on the scene three stories above the street in an apartment building.

Some First Platoon guys were yelling, "Come out with your hands up and you won't be harmed." Several Spanish speakers were helping with the language.

My attention abruptly shifted from the scene above the streets when a sobbing woman pulled at my arm and pointed down the alley, pleading in Spanish. I turned to one of our Spanish-speaking soldiers.

"What's she saying?"

"She says that her eleven-year-old son has been shot in the chest by the PDF and needs help," he replied.

"Where is he?"

"Down the alley. She will lead us to him."

"Okay. Take two men and see if you can carry him out here," I instructed. They came back supporting a nervous, wide-eyed boy. The woman opened her son's shirt and exposed his chest. Directly over his sternum, a purple protrusion the size of a grapefruit jutted out, with a small hole at the apex where the bullet had entered. A steady trickle of brown blood ran down the boy's stomach, and the first signs of infection were setting in.

"My God!" I exclaimed. "Doc! Where is Doc?" One of the men ran and grabbed the medic, while the yelling up on the third floor of the apartment building grew more intense.

As Doc ran up to us he surveyed the situation. Shaking his head he conceded, "Sir, I'm no surgeon and that's what this kid needs."

Frustrated, I asked, "Well, what can we do for him then?"

"Not much, I'm afraid. Tomorrow Brigade is supposed to set up the mobile aid stations, and he can get help there. Until then the only people we medevac out are American soldiers. I'll give him some Motrin for the pain and clean him up, but that's the best I can do."

Feeling helpless and angry at the PDF for their cruel and torturous mistreatment of the people, we apologetically told the woman about her only recourse.

Meanwhile, the crowd cheered wildly when the last two PDF soldiers came out of the building with their hands up in the air. The people jeered at their former oppressors, cursing and spitting at them as we escorted the prisoners out.

"Viva Bush!" they shouted.

"Ya know," said Grimshaw as we walked back to the hotel. "A fella could get used to this. Staying at the finest hotel in Colón, swooning in the love and admiration of these people."

"Well, not me," countered Lancaster. "Ain't got no money, ain't got no hot chow, ain't got no woman, and ain't got no booze. Now how in the hell can you stand there and say you could get used to this?"

As we walked along the crowded streets in the heat of the day conversing among ourselves, we began to notice that a lot of the citizens had brand-new radios, sneakers, coats, and bikes. A cross reference revealed that the merchandise was from the connexes at the choke point; obviously the goods were stolen. Several times when we had to enter living quarters to search for weapons or former PDF and Dignity Battalion soldiers, we were amazed by all the new televisions, stereos, and refrigerators we found. One guy had seven televisions in his apartment. No doubt he was serious about watching TV.

Back in the coolness of our air-conditioned room at the hotel we remarked how guilty we felt for being so comfortable.

"Just think," said Grimshaw. "People actually pay to do what we're getting paid to do right now. This is a splendid vacation in a beautiful tropical land. We've got showers, air conditioning, TV . . . what more could we ask for? Right now my wife probably thinks I'm in hell, surrounded by wicked Panamanian demons and baby killers. Ha!"

"Now there ya go, not making any damned sense again," growled Lancaster, no doubt conjuring up a different set of mental images than those envisioned by the more optimistic Grimshaw. I figured that the truth was probably somewhere in between. We were still being threatened and in a dangerous, hostile environment but it could be worse — we could be hot, dirty, and wet. Our luck did not hold for long, however, as it began to rain early in the afternoon. It began as a slow drizzle but then developed into a violent downpour, drenching Staff Sergeant Moore and his men to the skin on their security patrol. Apparently, a would-be thief thought he could use the foul weather as cover while he robbed one of the shops that lined the garbage-strewn street. After all, who in their right mind would be out in weather like this? Unfortunately for him, he failed to recognize that the American grunt makes a habit of operating in the foulest of elements. Consequently, when Staff Sergeant Moore's squad caught him in the act of robbery, the thief found himself face-down in a mud puddle. His escalation of complaints resembled an early morning gargle by an elephant.

The remainder of the day was relatively uneventful. Two soldiers from the 1st Psychological Operations Battalion came by and dropped off some propaganda leaflets for us to post in conspicuous places when we went out on patrol. A Panamanian flag decorated the poster and it read:

DEMOCRACIA AL FIN
DESPUES DE LA TIRANIA
PAZ Y HARMONIA

Apoya al Gubierno del Presidente Endara

(Democracy forever. After the tyranny, peace and harmony. Support the government of President Endara.)

The Memorandum instructing us on the posters said:

1. The Democracy Forever poster is intended to displace growing local frustration over law and order problems from U.S. soldiers to "PDF Renegades" and "Para-Military Thugs and Criminals." It also demonstrates that U.S. and newly formed Panama Security Forces are active in the area where the posters are placed.

2. Place the poster on walls and poles throughout the operating area during normal patrolling operations. More than one poster may be placed on a wall and they should be used to cover enemy posters when possible.

3. Do not throw the posters on the ground or in the trash. This will have a counterproductive impact upon the local population. Do not feel obligated to use up all posters; return excess to the PSYOP LNO or higher headquarters.

It appeared that we would also be acting as political campaigners. The new job was not well received among the men.

Nightfall came and we continued to patrol in sector. A slight problem developed when some 7th ID soldiers accidentally shot across the boundary at a couple of our guys. This was not surprising since the streets used as boundaries all looked the same. We raised hell about it. The explanation from 7th ID was, "Well, we saw you had weapons, so we figured you were enemy." Closer coordination between our units fixed the problem. The importance of fire control and friendly boundaries can't be understated. Our commander made it very clear that any boundary violations or breaches in conduct would be severely punished under the UCMJ.

We had a couple of incidents where some of our troops became a little too friendly with the local females. This came to an abrupt halt when they were lectured on both the legal and biological consequences. "Men," said Sergeant First Class Crittenden. "You really don't want to bring back and give something to your woman that you didn't come down here with." He then went on to vividly describe the physical effects of several communicable diseases to some of the younger men. From then on flirting became non-existent.

The next morning, 24 December, the tactical operations center (TOC) for the battalion checked into the hotel with all their accompanying accouterments, including assorted radios, equipment, and office supplies. They occupied the wing opposite us. Soon after they arrived, LT Keith Parker and others informed me that some of the enlisted staff assistants were breaking into the hotel shops and rooms and taking things that did not belong to them. Their story was corroborated by other eyewitnesses. Immediately, I went to an accused soldier's room and banged on his door. I confronted him regarding the accusations, whereupon he pulled out a cloth and unwrapped it to reveal a handful of jewelry.

"I found it," he said.

"Oh? I have several witnesses that say you broke into the shops and rooms and stole it," I countered.

He just shrugged. I went to the TOC, told our intelligence officer about the incident, and placed the items in his custody. I told him anybody in our company found stealing would be relieved of duty on the spot and court-martialed. He nodded in agreement.

"Yeah, if we start taking things, then that makes us no better than the people out there," he said, pointing with his thumb toward the slum outside. "I'll see that it gets handled, Clarence."

A couple of minutes later the sergeant major charged down the hall and confronted me about the whole affair. He attempted to defend the soldier, saying that the soldier had found the items and had even attempted to turn them in.

"Bullshit, Sergeant Major," I said. "Have you seen the shops downstairs or the rooms on your wing? They're all ravaged since you moved into the hotel! Clean up your act!"

By now some NCOs had gathered around and Captain Dyer ran to the scene of the argument. For me the final straw was when the sergeant major addressed me by saying, "Listen here, Lieutenant," in a raised and threatening voice.

He took a step toward me. Normally I would have restrained myself. On more than one occasion I've suppressed the urge to beat the crap out of a disagreeable servicemember who implied that he would get physical in order to get a point across. I broke only once before; the rest of the times I just sucked it up and kept the anger at bay. But not this time. Maybe it was the pressure of the situation, but I exploded and jumped in his face, hoping that I could get him to put his hands on me so I could do a body lock and slam him to the floor. He backed down though, and walked off the other way.

Afterward I felt bad and wanted to apologize to the sergeant major for losing my temper, but the opportunity never seemed to present itself. I realize that such opportunities never occur by chance. They must be created.

Later that morning Don Brown and Steven Hagan brought us our mail and a Lieutenant Garcia, who would be working with us as a liaison officer for the newly created Panama Public Forces (FPP), or security apparatus. He was a former member of the PDF's Battalion 2000. An estimated 4000 or more former PDF soldiers had been sworn in under the Endara government as newly appointed members of the FPP. The assumption was that most of the appointees were untainted by the violence, corruption, and drug trafficking of the Noriega regime. Of course, we all knew that this was unlikely, no matter how carefully they screened the new deputies. Colonel Roberto Armijo, one of Noriega's closest aides who had stood by him through several coup attempts, was sworn in as head of the FPP. Many of Noriega's other cronies also filled important posts, even though they had broken with the strongman only weeks before U.S. intervention.

The FPP consisted primarily of former PDF officers wearing different loyalties. The prevailing argument in defense of them is that they are men who serve their country regardless of who is governing it and are still loyal to the nation at large. After all, everyone knows that professional soldiers don't get involved in politics but serve the nation as official government servants. Right? Wrong.

The officer corps had lived well under Noriega. He dispensed the country's dwindling resources to his top officials, and many citizens were aware of this. The people of Colón, who had been abused by the PDF and Dignity Battalions, despised and hated their oppressors beyond description. They mercilessly led us to wherever former Noriega loyalists were still in hiding. Revenge is a strong motive. The people were getting even.

Pockets of enemy resistance continued to hold out, and word trickled down that our occupation could drag on for a long time. One of the techniques used to speed things up was the "Guns for Money Program" that offered Panamanian citizens reward money for turning in weapons and ammunition. Suddenly, guns were coming out of everywhere as people sought to get rich quick. The memorandum describing the program read as follows:

UNCLASSIFIED
SUBJECT: MONEY FOR WEAPONS PROGRAM
1. THIS MESSAGE DESCRIBES THE MONEY FOR WEAPONS PROGRAM, WHICH WILL BE IMPLEMENTED BY ALL ADDRESSEES AS SOON AS POSSIBLE.
2. THE SUBJECT PROGRAM WILL PROVIDE PAYMENT IN RETURN FOR WEAPONS OF THE PANAMANIAN DEFENSE FORCES

(PDF) (TO INCLUDE REGULAR FORCES, DIGNITY BATTALIONS, TRANSITO POLICE, CENTURIAN POLICE, AND DOBERMAN RIOT POLICE). PAYMENT AMOUNT PER WEAPONS TYPE IS AS FOLLOWS: $25 FOR SUFFICIENT AMOUNT OF AMMO; $25 PER GRENADE; $50 PER RPG GRENADE; $100 PER PISTOL; $125 PER SHOTGUN; $150 PER AUTOMATIC RIFLE; UP TO $5000 PER ARMS CACHE (DEPENDENT ON SIZE). TO QUALIFY FOR PAYMENT WEAPONS MUST BE DELIVERED BY THE WEAPONS DONOR TO DESIGNATED TURN-IN POINTS.

Initially, the Guns for Money Program worked well, but as time went on it developed into what we came to call the "Hatfields and McCoy" syndrome. Just to get us to harass him, a group of Panamanians would claim that a disliked neighbor was a member of the PDF and had all sorts of firearms in his house. We went on several wild goose chases. Regrettably, we invaded the privacy of many citizens in search of alleged culprits and their munitions. The search for Noriega and his cronies was so all-consuming that numerous innocent Panamanian citizens suffered unavoidable injustices. For instance, one afternoon Staff Sergeant Popp came strolling into the CP with a big grin on his face, chuckling to himself.

"Okay, okay. What's so funny?" asked Grimshaw.

"Well," responded Popp slowly, attempting to captivate his audience. "We just finished patrolling that rich neighborhood behind the hotel where Noriega supposedly had a summer house."

"Yeah," we all chorused.

"We went to the house," Popp continued. "It was full of holes. Looks like the SEALs hit the breakwater and fired through the plate glass window on the sliding door facing the ocean."

"So what," I said.

"Well, there was an old man, his wife, and three kids in the house. The SEALs dragged them across the floor and made 'em lay face down at gunpoint. They asked the old man where Noriega was and he told them, slowly shaking his head and pointing, that he was sorry but they had made a mistake and that Noriega lived in the house next door!" Of course, Staff Sergeant Popp had to dramatically reenact the whole affair for us.

We roared with laughter so hard that several of us toppled out of our chairs onto the floor, eyes streaming with tears.

"Hey, now that's what I call a high-speed pinpoint operation," jeered Grimshaw.

"Must have still had their damned masks on!" another man cried. "Couldn't read those house numbers."

Lancaster scowled and commented sourly in a biting southern accent, "The empty-brained, frog-legged bastards never did anything right and never would since God was a paratrooper, and they did not have his blessing to come from below the depths when the only honorable way was to jump from an airplane while in flight!"

In reality, the SEALs performed some difficult missions exceedingly well in Panama and have a unique area of expertise that is invaluable. I'm sure that they had horror stories to tell about us paratroopers too, and somewhere along the line God owned a set of scuba tanks. At Fort Sherman there was a wide variety of elite troops including paratroopers, light fighters, Rangers, Delta operators, SEALs, and Marines, all of whom treated each other with an unspoken respect. Stories were traded and it was beneficial to hear how other elite troops operated.

A call over the radio from the guards at the front gate sobered us up as the handset crackled.

"Bravo 6, this is Bravo 3-1. We've got four Lebanese guys out here that want to get back into the hotel to pick up their things. Over."

"Bravo 3-1, this is Bravo 6 Romeo," replied Grimshaw. "What things? Over."

"This is Bravo 3-1. When the 7th ID moved into the hotel these guys ran for it. Over."

"Roger 3-1, search 'em thoroughly and then escort them in, we don't want another Beirut infiltration. Over."

"Ah . . . this is Bravo 3-1. We don't have to search 'em—apparently they were caught with their pants down and are standing out here buck naked. Over."

The transmission broke for a moment, and then continued.

"Looks like they've been running around the streets for a couple of days like this, and they're kinda pissed off. Over."

"Roger. Send 'em up. Out."

Shortly after, the four Lebanese men, who were past the point of embarrassment, paraded upstairs. We escorted them to their room, whereupon they began to tear it apart, lifting up the carpet and ceiling tiles and pulling out $100 bills they had stashed. We just stood in disbelief while they collected their money. They got dressed and took off, leaving us some spiced coffee in gratitude for allowing them to recover their money.

Later, at 1705, GEN Maxwell Thurman, the commander of SOUTHCOM, came on television and announced that General Noriega had turned himself in to the Vatican Embassy in Panama City. A simultaneous cheer could be heard throughout the hotel as the news was announced.

"Tricky bastard," I thought. The strongman chose the holiest night of the year to turn himself in to the one place that could offer him sanctuary. A standoff developed with the United States putting pressure on the Vatican to hand over the strongman. Outside the Papal Nuncio, the 82nd Airborne Division sealed off the neighborhood and ringed the area with loudspeakers that blasted rock music.

At 1755, Carlos R. Outten, the second in command of the Colón Dignity Battalion, turned himself in to us at the hotel. He told us that over 900 Dignity Battalion members were still at large and hiding in Colón. All his comrades were waiting to see how he would be treated by us. He said that they wanted a fresh start under the new government but were afraid to give themselves up.

Lieutenant Colonel Moore watched from the balcony above the hotel lobby as we searched Outten. He directed us to allow the man to call his family and to offer them protection in case his comrades took action against them for treason. Outten called and his family came but said they would rather remain at their home.

We took Outten upstairs and offered him an MRE, for which he was very thankful. The man, unfamiliar with the rations, tried to consume the cardboard and all as we watched in amusement. With some help he managed to get at the contents and remarked how tasty it was. Popp and I looked at each other and knew that he had to be very hungry to make such a comment. He told us that the reason we were having so much trouble with pockets of resistance was because

LTC Daniel Delgado, commander of the 11MZ, had ordered Major Guardia of the Dignity Battalion to release all of the criminals in Colón and arm them in order to give American soldiers more trouble. The plan backfired, however, when the criminals turned against the Dignity Battalion members, anxious to get revenge on those who had imprisoned them in the first place. Outten spoke in broken English but was obviously well educated.

"The PDF trains the Dignity Battalion like your National Guard," he explained. He paused for a moment to down his cheese and crackers. "To be in the Dignity Battalion, you must first belong to the Codepadi, if you want any kind of job working for the government. We must swear allegiance to General Noriega to get in [the Codepadi], and then we get paid $100 a month."

He cleared his throat.

"But Noriega made us angry. He missed two payments. He came to have a meeting here at the hotel and told us to fight hard. We were afraid and angry. We had no money for Christmas. Most of us don't want to belong to the Codepadi but need the income." He looked up hesitantly, searching our faces for reaction before he continued. "When you attacked the other night we ran away. Everyone changed clothes and ran. We were very scared. We were not ready for anything like you. We are not that well trained."

"Did you know when we would attack?" I asked him, wondering how our OPSEC was.

"We did not think you would attack during the holidays," he answered. "We saw you coming into the city. You looked like evil demons creeping up on us in the night. None of us wanted to die, so we ran for our lives, terrified of you."

As he continued his story, I got the impression that he was making excuses for running. If they had only known how scared we were too, they might have stayed and fought. Although I doubt it would have done them much good. We would have pulverized them either way. The gap in training and technology was too great. Furthermore, these guys didn't seem particularly cohesive or dedicated to a greater cause.

A squad from Third Platoon had the job of escorting Outten to brigade headquarters for further questioning. They were delayed along the way when a hysterical woman came out of a burning building yelling "FIRE!" The second story of an old building had collapsed and a man was trapped under the debris. The squad dug him out and noticed that the woman was still screaming. After overcoming the language barrier, they realized that the woman's baby was still in the building. Evidently she didn't even know the man and couldn't care less about him. So the men went back in and rescued the baby.

Lieutenant Garcia of the FPP had gone out on several patrols during the afternoon and was scheduled to leave out again that evening with Staff Sergeant Moore's squad. Moore stomped into the CP. "Do I have to take that bastard with me?" he asked scornfully. "Earlier today he was with Sergeant Jennings and Sergeant Popp, causing trouble on the street. He abuses the people, pushes them around and calls them names. Shit . . . he's scared to death too!"

Before Garcia had gone out on his first patrol he came to the CP and asked for a weapon. We told him no. He got angry and stormed out. One of our guys heard him talking to his wife on the phone, telling her he was in the Ghetto with the 82nd Airborne and that we were a bunch of uncouth animals. Since our first impression of him was insulting, it was the lasting one. He became scorned and distrusted.

As we were discussing Garcia, Sergeant Gruber walked into the room to announce that Garcia was downstairs in the casino drinking and gambling. The commander was away at a briefing so I decided to go down and investigate. I took Sergeant Gruber and a soldier who could speak Spanish with me, armed. When we walked in, Garcia was standing in front of a slot machine mechanically pulling the handle. Half a bottle of bourbon sat on the bar, uncapped. Garcia reeked of alcohol.

I turned to my interpreter and said, "Tell him that there is no gambling or drinking and that the casino is off limits."

My interpreter translated, but Garcia just kept pulling the handle. Perhaps military discipline was non-existent in the PDF. Finally, fed up with his detached attitude, I grabbed him by both arms and shook him, yelling in English. He grunted in astonishment and gave me a look that indicated he was astonished that I had put my hands on him. I noticed for the first time how soft he was. His flesh had no rigidity and he was obviously in poor physical condition, unaccustomed to rigorous training and exercise.

When Captain Dyer came back, Garcia told him about the incident and said that I had treated him with disrespect that was inappropriate for one commissioned officer toward another officer. Captain Dyer supported me as second in command but advised me to treat Garcia like an officer. So Garcia and I entered into an unexpected and uncomfortable truce. I had no respect for him. I think he suspected that I felt this way and kept his distance.

The next morning, as I walked out into the company CP from the bedroom, First Sergeant Butler grumbled, "Merry Christmas." He was bent over, rummaging through a box in search of an MRE that suited his palate. There would be few other reminders that day that it was Christmas.

Later, out in the city we observed that the looting had grown out of control. I got the impression that the people were determined to make this the best Christmas they'd had in years.

Since about 90 percent of Panama's wealth is in the hands of 5 percent of the population, poverty is everywhere. That Christmas was a day of reckoning, with the distribution of wealth becoming a little more equitable.

Back at the hotel, a throng of kids playing in front of the gate begged for MRE handouts from the guards. A few women offered their favors to the men in exchange for a tour through the hotel. It seemed everybody wanted to get into the hotel, particularly room 108, the purported suite of Manuel Noriega.

As I walked into the lobby, Lieutenant Corrigan asked me if I wanted to go along on a patrol with him and one of his squads. As we walked in two columns along the narrow road that led away from the front gate of the hotel, children jumped and cheered all around us.

"Gringo, Gringo!" they yelled. I had thought that the word was derogatory. Maybe it was usually, but not this time.

They offered us what little they had in the way of food and drink, holding our hands as we moved. Most of the men were a little jittery and only allowed their left hands to be held while the right hands supported their weapons, with index fingers on the triggers. The kids passed out all sorts of greeting cards to the soldiers. Evidently they had broken into a gift shop that sold Hallmark cards. I still have a Mother's Day card and a birthday card that were given to me by a tiny little girl.

As we rounded a corner a sudden movement caught my eye. A small boy jumped out and pointed a pistol directly at me. I hit the sidewalk, simultaneously charging my weapon and rolling into the gutter behind the curb. I quickly drew a bead on him, ready to squeeze the trigger. He just stood there smiling and looked at me, eager to see if there was more to the game he thought I was playing. I got up, angry and shaking, to take his toy gun away, but he dashed down the alley. Had it been night, I probably would have killed the boy before realizing he was just a kid with a toy gun. I hoped that no one else would make that mistake.

As we continued to patrol, a toothless old man stopped us in the street and pleaded for us to come with him. He claimed that he knew where some PDF soldiers were hiding weapons. We followed him to a four-story apartment building. We left most of the squad outside to provide local security and support while the rest of the squad, Lieutenant Corrigan, and I followed the old man into the building. The ground floor was flooded with about a foot of stagnant water. It was completely dark. There was no electricity.

The stairwell was narrow and crowded by the occupants of the building who came out to investigate the commotion we were causing. We cleared every room in the building, one at a time. A sense of guilt crept over me as I realized we were invading the privacy of these people. We were invading their homes. However, the nerve-racking ordeal of being so close to so many potentially threatening people kept me focused on the task at hand.

Lieutenant Corrigan had the 9mm pistol. He knocked on one door where there was no reply. Several more courteous attempts coupled with the old man's urging to shoot the door down finally prompted Corrigan to turn the handle. He stood off to one side, and I took cover behind the railing along with Sergeant Jennings as we pointed our weapons at the door.

"Okay, here goes," breathed Sean as the door ominously squeaked open.

"Whoops," I said, amazed by what the open door revealed. A young fellow was poised over a naked beauty. We stood staring at the couple, and soon everyone in the hallway was staring too. It was an uncomfortable moment for the couple and for us, but Lieutenant Corrigan, ever mindful of his duty, proceeded to enter the room. He clutched his 9mm pistol, still expecting to find a bad guy.

"Excuse me," he murmured to the couple as he lifted up the covers on the bed and poked his head underneath it to see if anybody was hiding. I couldn't help but laugh, so serious was he in his pursuit as he crept about the room like Inspector Clouseau in the "Pink Panther" movies. After we finished our search, we apologized and excused ourselves from the room.

The building was empty, and the old man tried to get us to follow him again. He was playing the Hatfield and McCoy game, and we weren't interested.

Walking back toward the hotel, we turned down a street bordered by a series of shops that were now inhabited by families. Entire jewelry stores were completely cleaned out with broken glass everywhere. It must have been total chaos here at H-Hour.

Outten had told us that H-Hour in Colón was a nasty affair that shattered the bonds of customary law. Violent mobs ran rampant, raping, looting, and shooting anyone who crossed their path. It reminded me of Cornelius Tacitus in *The Histories*, who described the Flavian Army as it approached the city of Cremona in 69 AD. At the time it was a great scandal because a Roman legion had sacked an unprotected Roman city. Colón, too, had been sacked, by former PDF, Digbats, and even its own citizens.

The following day, Captain Dyer, Sergeant First Class Crittenden, Grimshaw, and I took chow to Second Platoon. We were distracted by the sounds of shots over by the connexes. About thirty Panamanians were stealing winter jackets. One guy was wearing two when we arrested him. He made no attempt to remove them in the 100-degree heat. One fellow was riding his girlfriend around on a newly stolen bike, wearing his newly stolen sneakers and winter jacket, listening to his newly stolen radio. He was so proud of himself. She was proud too.

After we rounded up the looters and linked up with the MPs, who trucked the offenders away to a detainment camp, Captain Dyer received a call from higher headquarters saying that we had to assist a bank manager in transferring funds from a local bank to a secure place across town in the Free Zone.

The Citibank of Colón is just northeast of the DENI Headquarters we had attacked. The bank manager showed us a safe that had been broken into. Over $250,000 had been stolen from it.

"Will you look at that?" I whistled to Crittenden. Someone had taken an ordinary claw hammer and beaten through six inches of concrete and steel to get at the money.

"The son of a bitch had to have been on drugs to stand there and do that," said Crittenden. "Man, he must have been at it all night. Not a bad day's pay, though. I bet he's in South America somewhere by now."

There was another safe, a Diebold made in Canton, Ohio, that had withstood an attempt to breach it. The bank manager asked how we would get the money out. We considered using C4 to blow it but figured that the money would probably be destroyed. Her husband had borrowed an acetylene torch but didn't know how to use it. When it was discovered that a private in Second Platoon had once been a professional welder, he was pressed into service. He worked intensely for about half an hour before he cut a hole large enough to pull the money bags through. We loaded it up on the Humvee and drove it to the Free Zone where it was secured.

Back at the hotel, Lieutenants DeMoss and Bennett stood examining the day's catch of weapons. Lying on the floor were an AKM47, a sawed-off shotgun, an FLN, and a Thompson.

"All in a day's work," DeMoss remarked.

We were also informed that one of the hotel managers came by while we were gone and pulled $5,000 out of the freezer and another

$7,000 from a secret compartment in the bar. News also arrived that one 7th ID soldier had been knifed while on patrol and another had sustained a broken collarbone in a beating. This news was just another indication of how dangerous things still were. We weren't taking any chances however, and never traveled in anything smaller than squad-sized elements. We could have broken down into fire teams and gotten more rest, but that would have been comfortable, and too much comfort is what gets soldiers hurt.

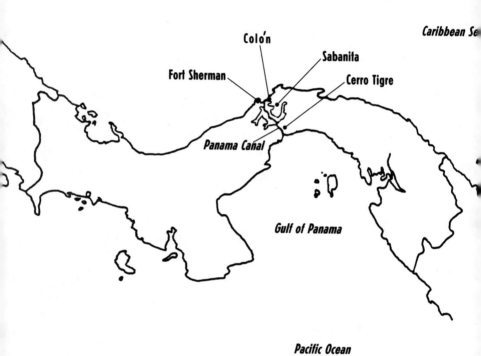

Caribbean Se

Colón

Sabanita

Fort Sherman

Cerro Tigre

Panama Canal

Gulf of Panama

Pacific Ocean

Guardians
Building the Peace

The next morning, December 27th, we were instructed to collect all of the AT4s, hand grenades, claymores, and LAWs and keep them at the company level. Soon they would be turned in altogether as we assumed the role of Guardians, entrusted with the task of aiding and assisting the local populace along the road to recovery. The principles of military necessity, proportionality, and the avoidance of unnecessary suffering translated into using force only when we were threatened to the point of losing life or limb. Not even looters would be fired upon, as it was not deemed worth shooting someone over merchandise.

Memorandums were distributed to provide soldiers with a "civil affairs checklist" of various public facilities, services, and installations. We were to report on a region's sewage system, electricity, water and food supply, medical coverage, fire-fighting capability, garbage disposal, and a whole array of systems that make civilization possible. Wherever possible, we assisted in re-establishing these systems. This memorandum, addressed to the soldiers of the 7th ID and signed by MG Carmen J. Cavezza, illustrates the transition to the Guardian role.

TO ALL LIGHT FIGHTERS:

You have won the battle. Our tough training has paid off. Now more challenges face us. We must do our part in neutralizing the last remnants of resistance. We must also help build the new government of Panama.

In our warfighting you have displayed constraint, self-control and fire discipline. When the enemy chose to fight, you defeated him decisively and aggressively.

I am proud to be a Light Fighter and command such good soldiers. We must now renew our enthusiasm.

● Don't relax your security—look like Light Fighters. I expect you to remain in our field uniform.

● I expect you to maintain your field uniform in accordance with the Light Fighter policy.

● Shave daily, keep your equipment clean and ready to use.

TO THE LEADERSHIP:

As I visit units, I am concerned about bunching up and poor security. There will be snipers around until we leave. Any leader who allows his soldiers to relax and get killed or wounded is responsible because of benign neglect.

Safety must be constantly emphasized. Remind them of safety problems. I want no incidents.

● Souvenir-takers will be court-martialed.

● Treat the Panamanian people with respect and be considerate of their property.

● Be professional with bad elements.

● Always account for your people.

● Don't compromise your integrity.

This means I expect you to maintain the Light Fighter image you have built. I will not accept anything less.

This memo indicated the change in military posture but also stated explicitly that security could not be sacrificed. This is the type of command guidance we needed. We would assist in the process of "rebuilding" at our level by supervising the food distribution point and medical aid station that had been established in our sector. We were not particularly overjoyed or enthusiastic with the task, but nevertheless we made our contribution.

First Platoon had the job of managing the food distribution point. When Lancaster and I pulled up in the Humvee early that morning a line had already formed that was more than four blocks long.

"Hey Jim," I waved as we rolled to a stop. "Expecting a riot this morning?"

"Naw, it's pretty quiet, mostly women and children."

We both turned our heads and focused on a robust middle-aged woman who approached us and began praising American soldiers.

"You are good boys," she said. "Why don't you beat the PDF like they beat everybody else, though?"

"Because," Jim DeMoss replied. "It's against our law to. It would make us no different from them." She couldn't understand and quickly changed the subject when she spied Staff Sergeant Lancaster puffing a cigarette.

"Hey you—hey, good looking!" she called as she smiled at him.

"No, no—now wait a minute, ma'am . . ." he protested.

She cut him off and pleaded, "I make good Panamanian wife—you be lucky to have me." Lancaster shook his head sharply.

Jim and I cracked up as we watched him squirm. She finally gave up trying to marry him and said she would settle for a ride in the Humvee instead. This didn't seem like too demanding a request, but she disappeared before we had a chance to reply. We drove past the aid station before moving back to the hotel. Everything seemed to be going just fine.

After lunch I accompanied Lieutenant Corrigan and a squad from Third Platoon on patrol. We were down by the connexes when suddenly everything was in chaos. People were running out of the choke point carrying cases of Russian vodka. We surrounded them and forced them to put down the stolen goods. I stopped a Scandina-vian man and his family who were carrying a case toward their boat, which was moored at the dock. They claimed they had purchased it and I waved them on, unsuspecting.

Abruptly, I caught myself. They were well dressed, Caucasian, and appeared harmless. Yet I realized that the only reason why I had let them go was because they were white, spoke English, and had nice clothes. Angry at myself, I ran after them.

"Stop!" I yelled. "Put down the vodka and follow me."

The man became upset and feigned innocence. He smiled a crooked grin and said there must be some mistake.

"Yeah," I said. "I just made one. You're under arrest, pal. Follow me. You're gonna join the rest of the hoods." I placed him under the care of the squad leader, who was guarding the rest of the detainees.

Meanwhile a PCC truck pulled up and two men clambered out and began collecting cases of booze. It was an inside job. These jokers worked on the docks and were stealing the goods. Corrigan ran out to stop them, cussing madly. The thieves climbed back into the truck and drove straight at him!

I locked and loaded my weapon, took aim, and fired over the top of the cab. My front sight post dropped on the driver when the truck stopped and the men got out with their hands up. Corrigan was cussing because his feet got wet when he accidentally stumbled into a puddle. We breathed a sigh of relief and collected the PCC employees with the rest of the crooks.

While we were waiting, Corrigan became very upset and broke every bottle of Russian vodka we had confiscated in front of a crowd of several hundred people.

"Nobody gets it!" he bellowed as he smashed the bottles on the pavement.

"What a waste," lamented the squad leader, looking on in amazement. A five-ton truck arrived and whisked the thieves away. With them were "Hans and Gertrude," the lovely couple from Denmark.

The next morning we collected all of our things and headed back to Fort Sherman. Rumor had it we were going back to refit for our next mission. Leaving the hotel that had been as dear to us as any home was a bitter pill to swallow, but before long we were bouncing down the narrow streets in a five-ton truck waving farewell to all the citizens in our sector. Narrowly escaping death, by way of an insane and speeding driver, we pulled into Sherman shaken up but unscathed. Two items of immediate concern were the 100-percent-sensitive-items inventory and the submission of applications for awards for deserving individuals.

That evening we ate a feast of broiled steaks, fresh biscuits, sautéed vegetables and steaming hot coffee in the mess hall. It was the first time that Lancaster didn't have something derogatory to say about the chow.

The morning of the 29th found us aboard an LCM, chugging down the Canal toward Gamboa. The craft leaked badly and the men scrambled to retrieve their rucksacks from the forward end of the craft where the flooding seemed to be the worst. Much cussing and arguing followed about the new arrangement of rucks, mostly over whose ruck was on the floor and whose ruck would go on top. A private was complaining loudly that his rucksack didn't have a waterproof bag and needed to go on top of the heap.

"Stop your fussing!" bellowed his squad leader. "This whole damned country is wet. It won't make no difference if your ruck is too!" The NCO turned his attention back to his previous conversation, removed his helmet, and placed it on his own rucksack. He was bragging about an affair he had once when the private slyly poured half a canteen of water into the NCO's unprotected kevlar. When the NCO finished his tale of his amorous exploit he crowned himself with a helmetful of water.

"Behold," the private declared gleefully. "It's Sergeant Wethead. Don't worry, Sarge, everything in this damned country is wet anyway and it won't make no difference if your head is too." His revenge made us all laugh heartily.

The engines roared and the water churned as we pulled into the docks at Gamboa. The boatswain manipulated the controls and we glided perfectly into the embankment where we off-loaded. Delta Company arrived by truck convoy and we swapped places with them, as we were to relieve them at Madden Dam. Captain Dyer went with the first lift to the dam while I went to the TOC to see if there were any changes in the rules of engagement.

"XO, see if you can get some more maps," Captain Dyer told me. "Oh, and see if there is any mail." I went to the TOC and procured both items before going to Madden Dam.

For the most part, the mission was boring. Traffic control was not our specialty but we took it in stride, knowing that we only had to do it for a day. We were spread out, with Second and First Platoons positioned at critical intersections to block access to the dam while First overlooked the facility.

In the afternoon, I took one of the PCC pickup trucks out to the main checkpoint manned by Third Platoon. When I arrived, a large, muscular fellow who claimed that he was a retired Special Forces operator was complaining that the previous commander owed him some money for weapons he had turned in. When we told him we didn't know anything about it, he raised his voice angrily.

"Listen, pal," I said, "you'll have to come back tomorrow because we don't know what you're talking about."

He whined even more, gesturing in a threatening manner with his big arm. "You owe me . . . I'm SF. You can't teach me anything about the military—I'll show you."

He continued for a minute longer before I finally got fed up with him and did some threatening myself. "You know, for a fella that can't be taught anything, you fail to recognize that I've got the gun and you don't and that you're pissing me off right now!"

I dramatically charged my weapon, an action which seemed to convince him that I was thoroughly insane and deadly serious. I went on in my best Clint Eastwood accent, speaking in a low husky growl, "Now you got exactly ten seconds to get in your car and drive away, unharmed."

I started to count out loud, slowly, squinting my eyes. The only thing I was missing was a stubby cigar and some western background music. He didn't call my bluff and quickly hopped into his car, mumbling protests. We all laughed. Later, we found out that the guys from Delta Company called him "secret agent man" and that he had actually gone out and captured some enemy personnel and weapons.

The evening passed without incident except when we received a radio transmission saying that General Johnson and Lieutenant Colonel Moore would be paying us a visit the next day.

The next morning the Huey hovered momentarily before it settled onto the small clearing next to our CP. We stood rigidly at attention as General Johnson, Lieutenant Colonel Moore, and CSM William McBride walked briskly up to us. We were ready to answer questions about the tactical situation and were surprised when they wanted to know whether we were getting any mail.

Captain Dyer took the general and the sergeant major around in the Humvee to inspect the troops. When they arrived at First Platoon's location, the general spoke with CPL Kevin Murphy for a moment and then turned to the sergeant major and said, "Now there's a future Sergeant Major of the Army. He has already led a squad in combat as a corporal."

Murphy thought about the compliment for a second and then respectfully responded. "Well, Sir, I had actually planned to get out and try something else."

Everyone chuckled in amusement. After the visit the general and the sergeant major lifted off in the helicopter with Lieutenant Colonel Moore and waved goodbye.

"Wonder why he wanted to know about the mail?" someone asked.

"Probably cause he ain't been gettin' his," responded Staff Sergeant Lancaster. "He's just seeing if something in the system is broke before he chews them mail clerks out for not getting the mail out to us troops."

Actually, the mail flow was pretty steady and most guys got letters on a regular basis. When we deployed back to the schoolhouse in Gamboa there was even mail addressed "to whom it may concern" from "a concerned citizen." The first sergeant, the commander, and I tore into these letters, since we weren't getting much other mail. Soldiers love to hear from home. They want to know that somebody cares about them and what they are doing. The fact that it was Christmastime made us even more nostalgic about home than usual. My favorite letter was written by a small boy from Pennsylvania. It said:

> Dear American Soldiers,
>   Noriega is one word you prob[i]ably heard one too many times. I wish you all the luck in the world to find him. If you find him, GUN HIM DOWN! That man is like Hitler in my mind. I hope that man is sat on trial with a bullet through both eyes. We will keep you in are hearts always. We all will pray for you.
>   Good Luck always.
>   I live in PA!
>   Make his last sight a look down a gun barrel!
>
>   Good Luck.

The letter was accompanied by several drawings that clearly depicted how we were to accomplish the boy's desires.

The remainder of the night we spent in the old schoolhouse was uneventful. At 0300 hours we awoke and readied ourselves for our return trip to Cerro Tigre, where we would conduct police call. Our job would be to clean up the mess that had resulted from looting and vandalism by units that had occupied the logistics site after our initial attack. The men were quite upset and complained loudly.

Cerro Tigre was a mess. Garbage was scattered everywhere. Uniforms and equipment had been ripped out of boxes and strewn all over the compound. Somebody had broken into the storage bins at the mess hall, consumed what they wanted, and left the rest to rot. It was difficult to accept that soldiers were responsible for these offenses. All of this was in clear violation of the directives that had been issued to us from higher headquarters, yet here was the evidence, glaring and undeniable. Anger turned to disgust and then shame. Grudgingly, we cleaned the place up and reestablished some semblance of order.

We spent one more night in Gamboa and then moved north to Sabanita early the next morning. Sabanita is a small town about ten kilometers east of Colón just south of Puerto Pilon. Although located right on route 20, it was not a priority target during H-Hour. We were instructed to occupy a police station there that had been assaulted by the locals on D-Day. Some MPs were attached to us. When the citizens had heard that the rest of Panama was in revolt, they took it upon themselves to attack the DENI headquarters and force out the PDF and Digbats who occupied the station.

The commander divided the town into sectors and we began patrolling. First Platoon kept getting reports about a man in the sector who was accused of working for Noriega. Closer investigation revealed that the man was Rafael Ceballos, accountant for the Noriega administration. A search of his house produced a variety of military weapons and communications equipment. First Sergeant Butler, Lancaster, and I hopped into one of the vehicles that we had impounded and drove to the Ceballos residence. Some neighbors were standing outside the gate of the Ceballos estate.

One of the men acidly remarked, "Yeah, me and Ceballos had it out a couple of times. He put a $5000 contract out on my head once. Serves the bastard right. When we heard you guys were coming, we sealed off his house with wire and pungi sticks." The man continued to describe his defense in detail with a great deal of pleasure. He obviously had had some military experience.

By ordinary standards the Ceballos residence was incredible. Three huge satellite dishes sat majestically upon the well-manicured lawn. Some sort of high-speed antenna stretched skyward for at least thirty meters. The estate was enclosed by a metal gate and stone wall. The

These weapons were found and captured at Rafael Ceballos's house during our mission in Sabanita. *SPC James Barbour*

entrance into the courtyard was paved with hand-laid stone that had been polished to a glossy smoothness. A sunning pool sat off to one side opposite a driveway where a Mercedes and a Chrysler were parked.

The inside of the house was even more impressive. After glancing at the family being held at gunpoint on my way in, I walked into the living room. Original oil paintings hung on every wall, marble statues stood in every corner, and furniture that looked too comfortable to sit in filled the room. At the junction of the halls leading into the bedrooms, a fountain gurgled. It was sculpted to give the appearance of a waterfall cascading into a pool of tropical fish. Each bedroom contained a wide-screen console television that took up a whole wall. Just off the dining room was an entertainment room complete with a wet bar that could compete with any sophisticated nightclub in its selection of alcohol or decor.

"Hey, Clarence!" Jim DeMoss yelled from one of the rooms. "They've got a safe in here." Jim took the lady of the house to the safe and instructed her to open it. She did so, after some protest. Assorted documents and videotapes filled the safe.

We also found $5000 in cash and enough jewelry to fill a kevlar, all of which we recorded and left on the dining room table. Apparently Mr. Ceballos worked for a local corporation. His neighbor said that the corporation was somehow involved with the arms, drugs, and money connection between Cuba, Panama, and Colombia. Ceballos was allegedly responsible for the white-collar portion of the operation, laundering money while staying clear of any direct involvement himself.

The MPs took Ceballos back to the station and locked him up. An MI warrant officer came by and persuaded Mr. Ceballos to divulge the location of a munitions depot used by the PDF about three miles up the road.

We were excited by the prospect of doing something besides civil affairs work and wasted no time in piling into the trucks and rushing to the reported munitions location. We encountered no resistance when we arrived. Unfortunately, we did not know that Alpha Company had already checked the place out and reported its findings. Consequently, out of ignorance, we decided to breach the bunkers.

"Now what is the best way to get into these things?" asked Captain Dyer. We considered blasting the heavy metal doors with an AT4 but decided that it was too risky just in case the bunkers were full of explosives.

Instead we used a five-ton truck to ram the doors open. The driver was excited at first, by the opportunity to do something besides drive us around and sleep. Everyone stood back and he revved the engine.

Crash!

The heavy door caved in as the bumper of the five-ton truck split the door wide open in one shot. Inside the bunker we found all sorts of plastic explosives, dynamite, det cord, and blasting caps. Most of the stuff was manufactured and shipped by Nitro Nobel Corporation from Sweden.

The rest of the explosives came from an American Company in Dallas. Records indicated that tons of explosives worth millions of dollars had been shipped. The det cord was the same stuff we had run into in the booby traps at the EOD site.

After crashing into the first bunker, the driver began to lose his nerve and the grin disappeared from his face as sweat poured from his brow.

"He ain't revving that motor so high now," chuckled Lancaster as we observed the truck daintily push the last door open. After we were done, First Platoon left a squad-plus to guard the place and we headed back to the police station.

We spent the next couple of days patrolling and mingling with the locals, who were so hospitable that they argued among themselves over who would feed us. Some of the men complained that they were getting fat. Some just complained.

"What in the hell are we still doing here?" asked Staff Sergeant Popp as he threw his kevlar down in disgust. "These people don't need us here anymore. We walk up and down the street like a bunch of assholes. The novelty is wearing off!"

This five-ton truck was used to breach bunkers full of explosives at Sabanita.
CPL Mark Ruiz

Explosives found inside the bunkers at Sabanita were identical to those used by the enemy to make booby traps at the EOD site. We found an incredible amount of explosives, from numerous companies worldwide. Some of the shipments were fairly recent. *SPC Danny Myers*

Popp, of course, knew better. We were still needed, but not in a way readily apparent to an infantryman. We were more like social workers, evaluating and providing assistance to the local population. Not that there was anything wrong with this role. The problem lay in the speed of our transition from the battlefield and the parallel changes in the rules we had to play by.

On January 3 we packed up and convoyed back to Fort Sherman. After turning in our weapons, we ate dinner in the mess hall and traded stories with the men in other units. At 2140 hours President Bush appeared on television and announced that Noriega had given himself up to U.S. authorities. He restated the administration's four original goals: to protect American and Panamanian lives; to exercise American rights under the Panama Canal Treaty; to restore democracy to Panama; and to bring Noriega to justice. Cheers of victory echoed throughout the barracks, and it occurred to me that we had taken this all very personally. But then what other way is there to take it? Our job was finished, and we were looking forward to returning home.

I stopped by the recreation room on my way back to the CP, dropped several coins into a machine, and got a soda. One of the men who had been wounded at Madden Dam was in there also, sitting off by himself and staring at the wall with a blank expression on his face. He looked up when the can of soda clunked out of the machine, and our eyes met.

His face twisted into a grimace. He had the expression of a man who had physically exposed himself to danger and suffered unjust consequences. No amount of consolation or sympathy from me or anyone else could put the man at ease with himself. He was marked by a peculiar sense of suspicion and resentment that radiated from him like a man who has been betrayed by someone very close. For an instant, I considered joining him at his table, but I decided against the idea. His manner did not invite intrusion. He had been burned badly and the blisters had not yet healed. It was painful for me just to look at him and try to feel what he was feeling. Regretfully, and feeling somewhat uncomfortable, I pivoted and walked out of the recreation room, acutely aware that he was staring at my back until I disappeared around the corner and headed up the stairs.

The guys were lounging around, polishing their boots or reading mail. The scene was relaxed and relatively calm until one of the guys exploded in outrage and began to cuss loudly and violently. He started to punch the wall beside his bunk and was panting like a madman. Apparently, the letter he had received from his sweetheart announced that she had found someone else in his absence.

"That no good bitch!" he screamed. "I'll show her when I get back."
Staff Sergeant Lancaster addressed the poor fellow with the voice of
experience. "Son, I know you feel like you been done wrong, and you
have. Don't think you're the first son of a bitch that's got a letter like
that. It's been happening to soldiers since soldiering began."

"Yeah, but Sarge, we were supposed to get married," lamented the
soldier.

"Well, it's a good thing you found out about her now and not when
it would have really cost ya," Lancaster replied.

I observed the scene and listened to the talk for a while. Everyone
seemed to reach the consensus that women were no good except for
mothers, grandmothers, and sometimes sisters.

I was bone tired. Ignoring the discussion, I crashed into my bunk
and slept deeply until dawn.

The following morning we formed up outside as a warm breeze
blew across the ocean and filled our nostrils with the salty scent of
seawater. The commander spoke to us, remarking how lucky we had
all been, and then we observed a moment of silence for our fallen
American comrades who had participated in the operation. It all
seemed so unreal. We had actually participated in combat. In our
sheltered American lives it had always been easy to ignore what many
around the world deal with every day. The ugliness of war had never
made an impact on us . . . until now.

Panama was an experience I shall never forget. Nor shall I forget
the men with whom I served. Not everyone was a hero. Not everyone
saw incredible episodes of combat. Not everyone was shot at. We
were just a group of men – soldiers – who had been called upon to do
our best. We did.

The first sergeant snapped me out of my daze. "Company Attention! Right Face! Forward March! . . . Quick time!" We set off on a
company run. Something was different this time. A sort of intangible
energy filled the air that we could all feel. We were all part of it. We
finished the run in record time, sweating profusely and breathing
hard. Nobody fell out. We all knew the rules.

Rules of Engagement

Implications for
the Future

Some people believe that current definitions of military professionalism can adequately assist the soldier in the type of abrupt role transition we experienced in Panama. But since the literature abounds with definitions that do not even seem to describe the same term, the concept of professionalism is elusive. Unfortunately for the grunt, this multiplicity of definitions reflects not only the prejudices of authors, but also the complexity of actions to which the term refers.

The thing the ground-pounder can never forget, however, is what distinguishes the military profession from all other occupations — what Harold Lasswell calls "the management of violence." This responsibility and area of expertise is all-consuming and unique to soldiering. It means being able to successfully lead your men into combat by virtue of technical competence and moral courage to accomplish a mission that most people would never attempt. This can only be accomplished by realistic and relentless training that is based on sound military doctrine. Unfortunately, when soldiers train constantly without ever actually going into combat, the edge can begin to dull. The challenge becomes routine, and good training may turn into bad training, the results of which can be catastrophic.

It is not impossible for a leader of troops to distinguish between good training and bad training, but the two can appear quite similar. Both types of training can follow unit mission training plans, and blocks can be checked and buzzwords used to assure superiors and subordinates that a unit is proficient. The difference between good training and bad training lies in the philosophy that governs it. Good training recognizes undeniably that war, of which combat is the central act, is a distinct possibility and that men engaged in combat either kill or are killed based on how well they are trained. Bad training, on the other hand, is something done from 9 A.M. to 5 P.M., where leaders fail to assume full responsibility for the lives of their soldiers.

Good training recognizes only one standard — the combat standard — and is derived from mission analysis and contingency plans solely focused on preparing for combat through tough, realistic, performance-oriented tasks. Conversely, bad training gives no consideration to the next conflict, but only occupies space on the training schedule and follows whatever standard happens to be convenient at the time.

Good training hurts like hell and is conducted under stressful conditions where critical combat and survival skills are deeply impressed upon the mind. Exposure to hunger, thirst, fatigue, extreme cold and heat, and other discomforts familiar to the grunt on the battlefield places demands on the decision-making process of leaders and soldiers alike, enabling them to react quickly in combat.

Since no conflict is ever completely foreseeable, military doctrine, an evolving body of knowledge and practices about our Army's organization, training, and fighting, is necessary to help us prepare for it. Doctrine is not derived in a vacuum. It is the distilled combat experience of our predecessors, coupled with assumptions about future probabilities, that is handed down to us so we might profit. While doctrine is not a substitute for rational judgment and careful examination of particular circumstances, it cannot be prudently ignored or overlooked.

I would hate to think of the consequences of Just Cause for our company had we not trained seriously and adhered to established doctrinal practices, especially in the area of urban combat. Although some aspects of the conflict may force us to expand the skill structure of the American infantryman, particularly in the areas of conflict resolution in other-than-warrior roles, we still need a point of departure, and that is ultimately to "close with and destroy the enemy." To lose sight of this is to adopt a view of the world unsuited for an infantryman. No grunt worth his salt will tell you that his primary function is to prevent kids from stealing tennis shoes, help old ladies cross the street, break up domestic quarrels, or rescue babies from burning buildings—but we found ourselves doing all of these things in Panama.

If Operation Just Cause is any indication of future conflicts, then it is safe to assume that civil-military operations will play a critical role in them. The dimension of civil affairs already exists in U.S. military doctrine. It focuses on the relationships between U.S. military forces, civil authorities, and people of the nations in which the military forces are operating. In military doctrine, however, the operating procedures for civil affairs activities are utilized primarily by units other than the infantry. Further development and focus upon civil affairs operating procedures for infantry units may be one way to alleviate unnecessary stress caused by rapid role changes of infantry soldiers who are not typically trained in broader aspects of conflict resolution.

For the benefit of those who may be called to action under similar circumstances, we must reconcile the professional contradictions experienced by soldiers who deployed to Panama. Two major imperatives become clear. The first, actually utilized to an extent, is to complete the operation rapidly with a group of coordinated yet independent units, thus achieving complete submission of the enemy. Then, immediately following the operation, bring in enough qualified personnel to fill the roles required for mopping up and rebuilding. Operation Just Cause was over almost as abruptly as it began, and military police and civil affairs personnel were brought in, but the infantry remained because there were too few follow-on personnel to go around. Consequently, infantrymen were required to perform missions under unfamiliar circumstances.

The second imperative calls for expanding the skill structure of infantrymen and cross training them in other roles they might be expected to play. This is not to say that the warrior role should be anything other than "closing with and destroying the enemy," but cross training would assist the soldier on the ground in determining what he must do under conditions similar to those encountered in Panama. Abstract terms and theories mean nothing to a soldier who is threatened by deadly force. He needs and deserves a specific, concrete guide for action and plenty of good training to go with it.

MG William A. Roosma, when discussing the need for a permanent Joint Task Force similar to the one that engineered Operation Just Cause, said, "There is a whole range of missions that go with that." He was referring to a highly trained and disciplined rapid deployment force that must be versatile enough to conduct both commando raids and peacekeeping operations. If it is unity of command and the principles of surprise and speed that we strive for at the Joint Task Force level, then we need to refine our Mission Essential

Task List (METL) so it will prepare the grunt for a rapid role transition on the battlefield. We also need to provide the soldier on the ground with a set of standardized procedures that will expedite that rapid transition.

Concerns such as national interests, the American public, Congress, military strategy, and domestic and foreign opposition are far above the common soldier's sphere of awareness. He is not concerned with the political defense of American foreign policy but is worried about whether the guy standing under the streetlight in the blue coat and new tennis shoes has a gun. The typical grunt does not care about a blueprint for light force modernization or whether it is better to have heavy forward-deployed units or rapidly deployable contingency forces based out of the United States. Rather, he needs to know how the principles of military necessity, proportionality, and avoidance of unnecessary suffering bear upon his particular combat environment.

Who is the enemy? Who is an innocent bystander? When can I use force and how much force should I use? The answers to these questions vary according to the role of the soldier and the rules of engagement under which he is operating at a particular time and in a particular place on the battlefield. We owe the American soldier, who for future conflicts must be equally prepared to direct traffic and to close with and destroy the enemy, answers to these questions. But most important, after we determine the answers, we must be willing to train on them.

Glossary

A-bag. A canvas Army duffel bag used to carry or ship a soldier's extra uniforms or equipment.

ACE Report. A report prepared during or immediately after a battle, in which a subordinate unit reports the status of its ammunition, casualties, and equipment to higher headquarters.

Airborne. Technically, the term refers to any operation involving the movement of military forces and accompanying logistical support to an objective by air. The term is also used as an expression of acknowledgment by paratroopers.

Airmobile. Any type of operation involving the insertion, movement, or extraction of troops using helicopters.

AKM47. A Soviet-made 7.62mm assault rifle.

AMC. Air Movement Conference. A coordination meeting between a ground tactical commander and a pilot before the two conduct a joint airborne or airmobile operation.

AO. Area of Operation. An assigned sector of operation for a unit that has been given a mission by higher headquarters in a specifically defined area.

AT4. A man-packed, shoulder-fired, antitank weapon.

Backblast. The explosive action opposite the projectile launching end that results when an antiarmor weapon is fired. It is important to remember that both ends of the weapon are dangerous.

Battle Position. A defensive position on the ground that is selected on the basis of a terrain and weapon analysis that determines where a unit can both defend and attack.

Blocking Position. A defensive position used to obstruct hostile traffic along a likely enemy avenue of approach.

C4. A military plastic explosive used primarily for cutting or breaching.

Chalk. A term usually used to describe members of the same lift on an aircraft.

Consolidate. Consolidate and reorganize is a process that a unit conducts after an engagement with the enemy. It includes reestablishing the chain of command, redistributing ammunition, and providing security.

CP. Command Post. The nerve center of a unit, responsible for command and control.

DDT. Direction, Distance, and Terrain. A formula for navigation. Soldiers should always know which direction to move in, how far they have to go, and what the terrain should look like, based on a map reconnaissance before they move to their destination.

Det Cord. Detonation Cord. A tubular plastic explosive that resembles a clothesline. It is often used to set off larger charges or demolitions.

Digbats. Dignity Battalions. Panamanian units that were primarily locally organized militias that were not well-trained or well-equipped.

DZ. Drop Zone. A specified area where airborne troops and equipment are dropped by parachute from an aircraft.

Fire Control Measures. Directives given graphically by a commander to subordinate commanders in order to assign sectors of responsibility. In general, all control measures should be easily identifiable on the ground. Used to control subordinate units and prevent fratricide.

FIST. A fire support team provided by a field artillery unit to a maneuver/infantry company. The FIST chief is usually a lieutenant who plans and coordinates all indirect fire support assets available to the maneuver unit.

FPP. Panamanian Public Forces. The FPP replaced the Panamanian Defense Force (PDF) as the primary security apparatus after U.S. intervention. The newly appointed members of the FPP were sworn in under the Endara government.

Frag Order. A term used to describe a hasty order given by a superior command to a subordinate one, usually to change or modify a previous, more complete operations order.

Friendly. Term used to describe U.S. or allied units involved in the same or a related operation.

H-Hour. The specified time on D-Day when a particular mission is executed or the operation begins.

Humvee. Army's all terrain vehicle.

IMT. Individual Movement Technique. Includes three- to five-second rushes, high crawl, and low crawl that a rifleman uses when engaged in a firefight with the enemy. The purpose of IMT is to reduce exposure to enemy observation and fire.

Infantry. The military occupational speciality or branch that is primarily charged with closing with and destroying the enemy. It is also responsible for seizing and holding terrain by physically occupying it.

LAW. Light Antitank Weapon.

LCE vest. Load-Carrying Equipment vest. Worn by each soldier and used to hold magazines, canteens, grenades, and other equipment that the soldier needs to fight.

LCM. Military Landing Craft. A large metal barge that can transport a company-sized element across water.

LZ. Landing Zone. A specified zone within or near an objective area that is used for the landing of aircraft, usually helicopters.

Magazine. The cartridge that contains the ammunition for a weapon system. It feeds the weapon the rounds, and is reloadable and interchangeable with other weapon systems of the same make and model.

Medevac. Medical Evacuation. A process in which a unit extracts friendly and sometimes enemy casualties from the battlefield. It can include but is not limited to man-carrying, vehicular, or air movement extraction.

Mermite. Sealed metal containers that keep prepared or cooked food in a state ready for consumption.

MRE. Meal Ready to Eat. The current Army C ration used to sustain troops when the consumption of prepared food is not feasible because of tactical constraints. MREs are pre-packaged, self-sealed meals that can be stored, carried, and eaten by soldiers while operating in a field environment.

One-Third/Two-Third Rule. A formula that directs a headquarters to consume no more than one-third of the time between when it receives operational guidance and when the overall mission must be executed before it issues its guidance to subordinate units. This leaves two-thirds of the remaining time to the subordinate units to plan and prepare.

OPSEC. Operational Security. Procedures to ensure that vital operational information will not fall into enemy hands and jeopardize a future friendly mission. Measures taken to maintain security and achieve tactical surprise.

Overwatch. The tactical role of an element to support (by observation or covering fire) the movement of another friendly element.

PDF. Panamanian Defense Forces. Panama's internal and external security apparatus under Manuel Noriega.

PIR. Priority Intelligence Requirement. Information gained by reconnaissance that is deemed essential to support future operations.

PZ. Pickup Zone. A specified area used to pick up troops and/or equipment, usually by helicopter.

Security. Precautionary measures taken to secure a force from surprise danger while stationary or during movement.

SOP. Standard Operating Procedure. Techniques for conducting tasks endemic to a particular unit that are uniform and consistent throughout that unit.

UCMJ. Uniform Code of Military Justice. The system of military law as applied to all personnel who serve in the armed forces.

Further Reading

Bettenbender, J. and G. Fleming. *Famous Battles.* New York: Dell Publishing Co., Inc., 1970.

Clausewitz, Karl von. *On War.* Edited and translated by Michael Howard and Peter Paret. Princeton, NJ: Princeton University Press, 1976.

Du Picq, Ardant, *Battle Studies.* Translated by Colonel J. N. Greely and Major Robert C. Cotton. In *Roots of Strategy Book 2.* Harrisburg, Pa.: Stackpole Books, 1987.

Huntington, Samuel Phillips. *The Soldier and the State,* Cambridge, Mass.: Harvard University Press, 1957.

Hyde, Charles C. *International Law Chiefly as Interpreted and Applied by the United States,* 2nd edition. 3 vols. Boston: Little, Brown & Co., 1945.

Janowitz, Morris, ed. *The New Military.* New York: Russell Sage Foundation, 1964.

Kelsen, Hans. *Principles of International Law.* New York: Rinehart, 1952.

Marshall, S. L. A. *Men Against Fire.* New York: William Morrow, 1947.

Midgley, E. B. F., *The Natural Law Tradition and the Theory of International Relations.* New York: Barnes and Noble, 1975.

Osgood, Robert and R. W. Tucker. *Force, Order and Justice.* Baltimore: Johns Hopkins University Press, 1967.

Phillips, T. R., ed. *Roots of Strategy: The 5 Greatest Military Classics of All Time—by Sun Tzu, Vegetius, De Saxe, Frederick, and Napoleon.* Harrisburg, Pa.: Stackpole Books, 1985.

Rummel, R. J. *Understanding Conflict and War.* New York: Sage Publications, Inc., 1976.

Sajer, Guy. *The Forgotten Soldier.* London: Sphere Books Ltd., 1977.

Singer, Joel D. and Melvin Small. *The Wages of War, 1816–1965: A Statistical Handbook.* New York: Wiley, 1972.

Tacitus, Cornelius. *The Histories.* Translated by Kenneth Wellesley. London: Penguin Books, 1982.

Wakin, Malham M., ed. *War, Morality, and the Military Profession.* Boulder, Col.: Westview Press, Inc., 1979.

Weigley, Russell F. *The American Way of War.* Bloomington: Indiana University Press, 1977.

Wright, Quincy. *A Study of War.* Chicago: University of Chicago Press, 1965.

Index